Building Better Learning

An RSTU Perspective

By Simon Bridge,
Michael Malone
and Ken Webb

SERC

Building Better Learning
An RSTU Perspective

By Simon Bridge, Michael Malone and Ken Webb

Published in 2024 by
South Eastern Regional College
Castle Park Road
Bangor
BT20 4TD

Printed by
W & G Baird Ltd

ISBN: 978-1-0687425-0-7 (print)
978-1-0687425-1-4 (ebook)

Simon Bridge has worked both as the Enterprise Development Director in the Northern Ireland government's small business agency and as a self-employed enterprise facilitator. As an (amateur) academic he has explored the understanding and promotion of enterprise and has written papers and books about it. Since 2008, he has also been a Visiting Professor at the Ulster University Business School.

Michael Malone has worked in the further education sector for 40 years lately as Director of Curriculum and Information Services at South Eastern Regional College. An Electronics Engineer with degrees from QUB and Ulster University, he has won many national awards for the College. He has developed a Project Based Learning model based upon partnerships with the Basque Country, VET Colleges and applied the methodology successfully across the College.

Ken Webb MBE has worked in government and the private sector, covering infrastructure projects, national advertising campaigns, product research and international sales in the Agri-food industry and IT consultancy. A qualified teacher and Chartered Accountant with qualifications from four universities, in 2008 he was appointed as Principal and Chief Executive of South Eastern Regional College (SERC) which, under his leadership, has become Northern Ireland's top performing college, winning many awards including, for Ken, a Professorship at the Japan National Institute of Technology.

Contents

Figures

Acknowledgements

The authors wish to acknowledge that they did not work on this book alone and were helped especially by contributions from Brian Cummins and Michael Ievers from Stranmillis University College, Karen Bonner and Steve Pollard from Ulster University, Carol Fitzsimons from Young Enterprise NI and Natasha Lloyd from South Eastern Regional College. To them in particular the authors are very grateful.

The authors also acknowledge the support given by the Governing Body of South Eastern Regional College. The contribution made in supporting enterprising and entrepreneurial students at South Eastern Regional College by Professor Terence Brannigan OBE, Entrepreneur in Residence at the College, is deeply appreciated.

Foreword

Education stands at a crossroads. Yet while the world changes at dizzying speed, the UK education system's relentless focus on rote learning and examinations fails to deliver the skills, knowledge, and mindsets young people need to thrive in the 21st century. Indeed, it stifles them.

But change is afoot. Across the educational landscape, efforts are underway to transform the system. By offering a practical approach to more relevant and meaningful learning, this timely book is the perfect example. With an emphasis on integrating project-based and experiential learning with essential skills like problem-solving, creativity, and communication, Michael, Ken and Simon neatly outline how to cultivate more empowered students who are prepared for an unpredictable but dynamic and interconnected world.

The Edge Foundation has long advocated for deeper learning that connects classroom study to the real world, while nurturing a strong sense of purpose. We have seen first-hand the impact of this approach. Deeper learning is not just a UK phenomenon but part of a growing global movement. From the Academies of Nashville in Tennessee to XP School in Doncaster, educators worldwide are discovering new ways to create authentic, interdisciplinary learning. When students engage in projects, collaborate to solve complex problems, and connect the curriculum to the world beyond the classroom, they develop the skills, confidence and agency to thrive in life and work.

Drawing on the journey of South Eastern Regional College (SERC) in Northern Ireland, this book outlines how a vision for a better future for education - while ambitious and challenging - is entirely achievable. The efforts of trailblazing organisations like SERC and others have laid the groundwork for transforming education from an exam-passing exercise to an affirming experience that nurtures curious and adaptable lifelong learners.

As we collectively reimagine what's possible - not just in our schools and classrooms but across society - I know this book will make a valuable addition to any educator's arsenal. Its practical approach and focus on the learner will help many to create deeper and more meaningful learning experiences. The future depends on it.

Olly Newton, Executive Director of The Edge Foundation

Introduction

Our starting point

Often the education system in the UK appears not to meet the needs of people's lives today. One aspect of this, and the main trigger for the interest of the authors and contributors to this book, has been the demand for more to be done to educate people to be economically productive by helping them to be employable, to be enterprising and/or to be entrepreneurs who start businesses.

In Northern Ireland the contributors have been trying in various ways to respond to this - and this book seeks to draw lessons from that thinking and experience.

What is required?

Employability, enterprise and entrepreneurship have been discussed and analysed by many commentators but without coming to a common or widely shared conclusion. Even so, it is clear from examining what others have said that a key foundation for employability, enterprise and even business start-up is a shared set of what have been labelled transversal (T) skills or, at a higher level, uber (U) skills.

Transversal and uber skills are those skills needed for applications such as citizenship, coping with uncertainty, creativity, digital literacy, problem solving and decision making, self-management, working with others, and work professionalism plus emotional intelligence, critical thinking, leadership, and entrepreneurial thinking. They are not fundamentally knowledge-based but are clearly very useful and relevant, not just for economic activity but for many aspects of life. However, they rarely appear to be recognised, consciously included or systematically measured in the education provision.

Why have they not had the recognition they merit?

These transversal and uber skills appear to be overlooked for a variety of reasons including:

- The lack of an agreed label and definition hinders recognition.

- In circumstances where they are considered, the vocabulary used is loose and confusing - so discussing them is not easy.

- There is no clear acceptance of where they would fit into the education system.

- Schools, colleges and universities often cannot see how they could in practice be delivered.

- Unlike many other subjects, they cannot be assessed by traditional examinations while continuous assessment systems lack recognition and parity of esteem because they are not fully understood by educational establishments.

What this book wants to offer

Based on the various experiences of its contributors, this book endeavours to offer:

In Part I:

- An explanation of why exploring economic applications leads to T and U skills - plus a summary of what they are and why they are important.

- A defined vocabulary to describe T and U skills and their context.

- A suggested map showing how T and U skills relate to the more traditional components of education such as the basic three Rs (reading, writing and arithmetic) and then traditional school subjects (or S learning).

In Part II:

- Examples of how T and U skills can be delivered and an indication of the steps necessary to facilitate this.

- Suggestions and examples of how the acquisition of T and U skills can be assessed and recorded.

In Part III:

- Reflections (and some suggestions for further exploration).

What then?

It is hoped that this book will help to widen the recognition and delivery of T and U skills, but it is by no means the final word on this subject. Instead, it is offered to stimulate thought and practice in the hope that feedback from that will, in turn, lead to improved understanding and practice of this important aspect of education.

PART 1

A 'MAP' FOR A NEW EDUCATION MODEL

CHAPTER 1

A 21ST CENTURY EDUCATION?

Chapter Summary

In the UK long-term employment opportunities and a compulsory education system are two legacies of the Industrial Revolution. However, that education system is still essentially a Victorian model which, after basics such as the 'three Rs', endeavours to impart knowledge about a range of subjects to prepare its students for employment in the public or private sectors.

Indeed, one of the purposes of education is acknowledged to be economic but the world of work has changed with long-term job opportunities in large organisations becoming rarer and switching jobs and self-employed working becoming more common. Consequently, questions have been raised about the ability of the education system to facilitate this and to prepare people for 21st century life and work.

This book looks at what is now required, at what is being done in a Northern Irish example to facilitate this, and at a suggested perspective of the education system to show how this could fit with its other, more recognised, outputs.

Introduction

The OECD has observed that 'most 21st-century students are still being taught by teachers using 20th-century pedagogical practices in 19th-century school organisations'[1].

In the UK the legacies of the 19th century Industrial Revolution are said to include compulsory formal education and contracts of employment. Much production work, such as spinning and weaving, had been 'put out' (sub-contracted) to people to do in their homes. Therefore, when people were hired to work shifts on the new machines which had to be in factories where the power to drive them was available, contracts of employment were needed to confirm the agreement that they would turn up when they were required[2] - and education, which became compulsory in 1901[3], was needed to ensure that people were adequately prepared to undertake such factory employment.

Consequently, long-term employment at an employer's premises became the expectation and indeed aspiration for many people. Also, what has been described as the Victorian model of education continued in which a school operated like a factory to produce people with the knowledge and skills to be good industrial employees[4] or to work in other professions. However, more recently, the nature of work for many people has altered with jobs for life with large employers no longer being the norm and consequently the education needed to prepare for life has also changed.

The Education System

The UK still utilises the Victorian model of education and that is the system with which most people are still familiar. Its starting point is the primary school which endeavours to build the basic skills such as reading, writing and arithmetic (the three Rs) and which is followed by secondary school where, as a preparation for technical training or further/higher education, pupils are taught a selection of standard subjects such as the use of English, mathematics, history, geography, physics, chemistry, biology and one or more foreign languages.

Those students who do continue to sixth form level then study a selection of these subjects more intensively, often with the aim of securing examination grades good enough to get them into university where study is further specialised.

These school subjects are generally delivered separately, each in its own silo, through what is essentially a memory-oriented process imparting knowledge of facts and theories. The effectiveness of this teaching is measured by examinations which test for retained knowledge and in which good results are often the key requirement for the next stage of a young person's progression whether to university or to vocational skill training as an aid to progression in life.

It is convenient to accept established provisions, like this education system and the thinking behind it, as tried and tested and therefore appropriate to be accepted as the established way of doing things. However, 'tried' and tested' does not mean 'proven and pertinent' but nevertheless such thinking often becomes the conventional wisdom - as explained by Galbraith:

'To a very large extent, of course, we associate truth with convenience - with what most closely accords with self-interest and personal well-being or promises best to avoid awkward effort or unwelcome dislocation of life. ... Economic and social behavior are complex, and to comprehend their character is mentally tiring. Therefore, we adhere, as though to a raft, to those ideas which represent our understanding. .... It will be convenient to have a name for the ideas which are esteemed at any time for their acceptability, and it should be a term that emphasizes this predictability. I shall refer to these ideas henceforth as the conventional wisdom.[5]'

But conventional wisdom is often misguided and, according to Sir Ken Robinson, 'education has two main roles in people's lives: it should help them to develop their natural capacities and to make their way in the world around them'. But, says Sir Ken, 'too often, it falls tragically short on both counts.[6]' Nevertheless, many people in the education system (and especially it would seem those in the relevant government departments) appear to manage not to recognise this (so it then becomes an 'unknown known') and instead adhere to the conventional wisdom about education because that is convenient.

Consequently, in the UK the 19th century education model has not changed significantly despite this being the 21st century, and, according to a recent Times Education Commission report, the education system 'is failing on every measure'[7]. The report itself acknowledges that the reasons for that are complex and correcting them will not be easy. As has been observed, 'for every complex problem there is an answer that is clear, simple, and wrong'[8].

Further Examination of the Problem

What is the problem with education? The OECD, in assessing the future of education, reported in 2019 that:

'In the face of unprecedented challenges, including an exponentially faster rate of technological change, meaningful and relevant changes in education are urgently needed to achieve more inclusive and sustainable development for all, not just for the privileged few.' [9]

It has also been suggested by a former professor of education that 'for generations education has been biased towards narrow forms of academic ability'[10] and by a business school principal that 'highly specialised sixth form education ... tends to turn out literates who are innumerate and numerates who are illiterate'[11]. That education, and the social values behind it, have not supported industry and productive enterprise. Instead of thinking that with a relevant vocational skill they should be able to find a job and the alternative is unemployment, people should be prepared to see other possibilities such as creating their own enterprise. Nevertheless, it would seem that not many are being encouraged, or equipped, to do that.

While the industrial age required people to know facts and processes, this is not enough to thrive in life and work today. For example, there is a continuing economic drive for more business formation, innovation and growth - and therefore a declared need for people with the ability and preparation to contribute to this. While employers may not articulate what is missing, they complain that people finish education with paper qualifications but not ready for work. Employer surveys report that, while many people leaving the education system have the technical knowledge and skills required for industry, they need further development of work-related skills such as the ability to adapt to change and to work with others.

The Purpose(s) of Education

Education has been described as 'an *essentially contested concept* [with] a vast range of definitions, none of which is totally satisfactory'[12]. Various views have also been expressed on its aims depending, for instance, on the personal views or professional remit of the people expressing them.

An overall view is that offered by Bartlett and Burton in their book, *Introduction to Education Studies*, in which they suggest that the main functions of education are development of basic academic skills, socialisation, social control and maintaining social order, and preparing for work'[13]. Another is from Sir Ken Robinson and his daughter Kate who, in their book *Imagine If...*, ask 'What is education for?' and suggest that its core purpose includes the four basic elements of Personal, Cultural, Economic and Social.

These are not dissimilar to other proposals and it would seem that there is some convergence in views on ideologies and aims which might be encompassed in the diagram in Figure 1.1.

Figure 1.1 - The Aims of Education

Most such lists include a work and/or economic dimension and, in describing the economic purpose, the Robinsons point out that 'this is one of the reasons governments take such a keen interest in education: they know that an educated workforce is essential to creating economic prosperity'[14]. Indeed, it is noticeable that in recent years there has been an increasing demand, often stimulated or triggered by government interest and variously expressed, for education bodies to provide 'employability', 'enterprise' and/or 'entrepreneurship' education:

'Employability has become a buzzword that pervades everything from policy to learning outcomes'[15].

'It is ... likely that young people in education now will face greater economic uncertainty ... than did their predecessors. Against that background, all young people will need more enterprising skills and attitudes, not just to set up in business (or enter self-employment), but also to build their own careers and to stay employable'[16].

'Entrepreneurship has emerged over the last two decades as arguably the most potent economic force the world has ever experienced. With that expansion has come a similar increase in the field of entrepreneurship education'[17].

But this economic purpose is failed by the education system when it does not give students the sort of skills and abilities which they need to live and work well and which a healthy economy needs in its contributors. As Sir Ken Robinson has put it:

'Economic Education should enable students to become economically responsible and independent. ... But the world of work has changed so profoundly ... and continues to do so at an ever-quickening pace. We know that many of the jobs of previous decades are disappearing and being rapidly replaced by contemporary counterparts. It is almost impossible to predict the direction of advancing technologies, and where they will take us.[18]'

So What?

The current UK education system might, at least in part, have been developed to serve the needs of the industry that emerged from the Industrial Revolution, but that is by no means its sole purpose. It is clear that new demands are placed upon it:

- Society continues to require and seek enterprising individuals to solve future problems in an ever-rapidly changing world.
- Some of these individuals will be entrepreneurial and play a major role in driving change, seeking new opportunities and growth.
- Education has a role to play in developing and supporting those enterprising people and entrepreneurial individuals.

The students who receive such an education will also have a range of different needs:

- Some will be under the age of 18 and be in School or Further Education; the goal for many is to stay in education to obtain qualifications as a route to employment.

- Some under the age of 18 find the formalities, culture and environment of schooling impossible to cope with and will drop out and seek other opportunities. This non-conforming mindset is typical of an entrepreneur.

- Neurodiversity amongst children and adults will impact on engagement with formal education structures and they may require alternative support whilst in education. Neurodiversity can be seen as a driver of entrepreneurship.

- Some participants over the age of 18 will continue in education in a full or part-time capacity to seek further professional development and qualifications.

- Some individuals may continue to reject formal education once over the age of 18 but may avail of some short-term interventions associated with developing their knowledge and skills. Later, as an older adult, they may begin a journey in full-time education.

The analysis in this chapter suggests that in the UK the education system could do better to prepare its students for the needs both of life and work in the 21st century. However, the problems affecting education appear to be complex in that they are not limited to just a single aspect of it or the result of a single cause and effect process which can relatively easily be identified and corrected. Instead, they are due to a combination of interrelated factors which are not all susceptible to the same corrective measures. Therefore, to address this fully, a combination of improvements is likely to be needed which will take time to develop and implement.

But change is possible and, according to the OECD, in some countries improvements are being made:

"In the education sector, some changes are already emerging. Schools are no longer seen as closed entities in themselves, but as part of the larger eco-system in which they operate. ... Some schools have started to collaborate more widely with other organisations in their communities, ... where teachers and students can become familiar with the skills and competencies that employers and other community members deem critical.

'These schools aspire to operate with a curriculum that recognises the need for interdependence and broadens the goals of education to include "education for citizenship". Such a curriculum would recognise the differences between individual students and acknowledge that each student has different prior knowledge and skills, as well as different attitudes and values, and, therefore, may learn differently. Thus, curricula will have to be dynamic rather than static. They will have to allow for non-linear learning paths rather than expect all students to follow linear progressions along a single, standardised path. They will have to be more flexible and personalised to ensure that each student's unique talents are developed so that all students can realise their full potential.[19]'

In this situation the purpose of this book, informed by education experience in Northern Ireland, is to suggest how a start can be made to introduce improvements. In particular it explores two aspects of this:

- Starting with what has been identified as one aim of education, that of its economic contribution, it suggests what this should involve, describes efforts already being made to improve it and illustrates that with some practical examples.

- And, as a context for that, it offers suggestions for a paradigm or perspective for viewing education which helps to show where this approach would fit in with other aspects of education, what is therefore needed and where improvements can be made.

Having in this chapter attempted to outline the context, the following sections of this book seek to deliver that offering.

References

1 OECD, Future of Education and Skills 2030 - Learning Compass concept notes (OECD, 2019), p.9

2 P. Urwin, Self-employment, Small Firms and Enterprise, (London: The Institute of Economic Affairs, 2011) p.23

3 D. Matheson (ed). An Introduction to the Study of Education, (London: Routledge, 2015) p.216

4 M. Muthukrishna, A Theory of Everyone, (London: Basic Books, 2023) p.346

5 J. K. Galbraith, The Affluent Society, first published in USA 1958 (London: Penguin: 4th edition 1991)

6 Sir Ken Robinson and K. Robinson, Imagine If..., (London: Penguin, 2022) p.xix

7 Times Education Commission: Bringing out the best, Final report June 2022, https://lordslibrary.parliament.uk/times-education-commission-bringing-out-the-best/ (accessed 1 Nov 2023)

8 H L Mencken, from the original "there is always a well-known solution to every human problem - neat, plausible, and wrong" in 'The Divine Afflatus' in New York Evening Mail, 6 November 1917

9 OECD, Future of Education and Skills 2030 - Learning Compass concept notes (OECD, 2019) p.6

10 Sir Ken Robinson and K. Robinson, Imagine If..., (London: penguin, 2022) p.xxiv

11 P. Moore, 'Why industry has such difficulty attracting the best young talent', International Management, June 1986 p.53

12 D. Matheson (ed). An Introduction to the Study of Education, (London: Routledge, 2015) p.1

13 S. Bartlett and D. Burton, Introduction to Education Studies (London: Sage, 2016) p. 15/16

14 Sir Ken Robinson and K. Robinson, Op Cit, p.42

15 S. L. Hansen and K. Daniels, (editors), How to Enable the Employability of University Graduates, (Cheltenham: Edward Elgar, 2023

16 H. Davies, A Review of Enterprise and the Economy in Education, (London: HMSO, February 2002)

17 D. F. Kuratko, 'The Emergence of Entrepreneurship Education: Development, Trends, and Challenges', Entrepreneurship Theory and Practice, Vol.29 No.5, 2005, pp.577-597

18 Sir Ken Robinson and K. Robinson, Op Cit, p.42

19 OECD, Future of Education and Skills 2030 - Learning Compass concept notes (OECD, 2019) p.11

CHAPTER 2

EDUCATION FOR ECONOMIC ACTIVITY

Chapter Summary

As Chapter 1 has indicated, one of the purposes of education is economic: to equip people to participate in, and contribute to, today's economic activity. However, a perceived lack of this ability, often expressed as a need for people to be employable and work-ready but also to be enterprising and/or entrepreneurial, has been a significant factor highlighting the need for change.

This chapter reviews interpretations of the terms 'employability', 'enterprise' and 'entrepreneurship'. It shows that, although between them they might be thought to lead to the three outcomes of being employable, being enterprising and being able to start a business, they are not clearly separate and, as the terms are often used, there is considerable overlap between them and no consistent distinguishing definitions. A different perspective is therefore explored in the next chapter.

Introduction

As indicated in Chapter 1, one of the purposes of education is economic: to equip people to participate in, contribute to and benefit from economic activity in today's world. A perceived lack of this ability, often expressed as a need for people, not just to be 'work ready' and thus more 'employable', but also to be 'enterprising' or even 'entrepreneurial' (the three E's), has been a significant factor highlighting the need for change. This chapter examines that requirement to try to identify what is actually needed from education for this.

Before the 1980s, big businesses, and jobs for life within them, had seemed to be the expected norm in successful economies - and therefore the key educational need seemed to be for traditional job skills. But, at a time of rising unemployment, this perception began to change and 'enterprise' and 'entrepreneurship' were also sought in the belief that they offered a solution to economic woes by leading to new business start-ups. However, the ability of people to do the newer jobs that were created was also seen to be an issue, so 'employability' became another 'E' requirement.

If one of the recognised purposes of education is to enable students to make an economic contribution, both for themselves and to benefit others, then the most obvious manifestation of that might be supposed to be found in education for employability, enterprise and entrepreneurship. These are not particularly new words but their introduction to this field is relatively recent and these forms of education are being advocated and lauded by a variety of stakeholders - usually as if they were separate routes each requiring courses specifically dedicated to that particular purpose. But what are they and why has interest in them arisen?

To help to answer such questions this chapter looks at why and how interest in employability, enterprise and entrepreneurship has evolved and what that might mean for education. Also, for this, it explores the meaning and nature of each of those supposedly separate 'E' concepts.

There appear to be three main sources of interest in these concepts:

- a requirement expressed by employers for people with the skills and abilities needed to work productively in modern businesses.

- an economic policy desire of more business start-ups and growth and therefore for the people with the drive and ability to contribute to that.

- a view sometimes expressed that, as well as acquiring knowledge and/or skills in specific subjects, students also need the ability to progress in their lives by applying that learning in real and changing situations.

These might be labelled **'employability'**, **'entrepreneurship'** or **'enterprise'** but, not only does each of these labels, to a varying extent, have its own tensions, inconsistencies and flexible vocabulary, but also there are potential links and even overlaps between them - often as if the people using them have picked their own definitions.

'When I use a word, Humpty Dumpty said in a rather scornful tone, it means what I choose it to mean.'
Lewis Carroll

Employability: Interest and Interpretations

Possibly the easiest of the three Es to consider is 'employability'. A prime driver of this agenda has been the concerns of employers seeking suitable employees and employability has been viewed as being about enabling people, even higher education graduates, to get those jobs.

As one commentator put it: 'employability skills and graduate outcomes are often seen to be the purpose of a higher education institution (HEI). Yet HEIs are continually criticised for graduates emerging without the skills needed to be successful employees.'[1] Consequently it has been argued that 'in the past 30 years, HE has experienced an employability agenda that has advanced both in terms of knowledge and understanding, but also in significance, making employability a priority for universities'[2].

Employability has been thought to be helped by skills such as those required for creativity, self-confidence, problem-solving, critical thinking and communication - and it has also been linked to social capital. However, these are transferable skills which help people to be enterprising in any context and, as Hansen and Daniels note, 'historically, apart from a brief period in the 20th century, work for most people has often been project-based and at least partly self-employed'[3].

In the context of personal development, employability can be associated with being enterprising. But, from an economic development perspective, it has also been linked to objectives such as improved productivity and therefore to the skills supposedly needed to enable people to work more efficiently.

More Interpretations of Employability

A wider perspective is given by Yorke who describes employability as 'a set of achievements - skills, understandings and personal attributes - that make graduates more likely to gain employment and be successful in their desired occupations, which benefits themselves, the workforce, the community and the economy.'[4]

From an employer's perspective the Confederation of British Industry (CBI) has used the definition of employability as 'the possession by an individual of the qualities and competencies required to meet the changing needs of employers and customers and thereby help to realise his or her aspirations and potential in work.'[5]

However, Cheng *et al* conclude that:

- 'Employability depends on the capabilities of individuals, of intrinsic capabilities which relate to the person attributes and skills of the individual.

- Employability depends on the labour market and depends on the chance of finding and keeping different types of employment.

- Employability is linked to social capital. Those with lower social capital are less likely to have had the opportunity to engage with work experience and to develop employability skills.'[6]

Mason *et al* report that employers see employability as the readiness for work, 'the possession of the skills, knowledge, attitudes and commercial understanding that will enable new graduates to make productive contributions to organisational objectives soon after commencing employment'. With the reference to attitudes and commercial understanding, this suggests that employers see the requirements for employment as more than just subject knowledge[7].

It has also been observed that:

'You get into ... potentially difficult territory when you start to have those hard and fast definitions. ... [Employability] is different things to different people.'[8]

Enterprise: Interest and Interpretations

The term 'enterprise' became particularly popular in economic circles in the 1980s which was proclaimed in the UK to be the 'enterprise' decade[9], not least because of enterprise's supposed association with new businesses. According to an OECD monograph from that time:

'There are, in effect, two definitions of, or approaches to, the word 'enterprise' and the practice of it.

One, which can be termed a **'narrow'** one, regards enterprise as business entrepreneurialism, and sees its promotion and development within education and training systems as an issue of curriculum development which enables young people to learn, usually on an experiential basis, about business start-up and management.

The second approach, which can be termed the **'broad'** one, regards enterprise as a group of qualities and competencies that enable individuals, organisations, communities, societies and cultures to be flexible, creative, and adaptable in the face of, and as contributors to, rapid social and economic change.'[10]

Thus, two approaches to enterprise were acknowledged - only one of which linked it specifically to business start-ups.

Interest in small businesses, and in the people behind them, had begun to emerge in the 1970s but then grew considerably after 1979 when Birch revealed his research which indicated that new jobs came mainly from small businesses. As this was a time of rising unemployment in many countries and new businesses were understood to be a key contributor to economic improvement, governments wanted more of them.

In economic development circles, it was the narrower, business creation, interpretation of enterprise which prevailed although the term entrepreneurship was then also sometimes adopted and used synonymously with enterprise. Nevertheless, enterprise was the preferred term in the UK and, since then, there has been a policy drive for more 'enterprise' as the supposed source of new businesses. This view also gained traction in education circles as economic development funding became available for 'enterprise education' - although other views persisted, even in some supposedly 'entrepreneurship' circles.

An example of this is described by Bridge *et al* in their assessment of the Northern Ireland Centre for Entrepreneurship (NICENT) and its work in the local universities[11]. They reported that, while the funders of the programme may have expected a business creation outcome, many of the participating university departments and their students liked a wider view of 'entrepreneurship' which the authors of the report termed **'enterprise for life'** - as opposed to **'enterprise for new venture creation'**. Because it found that even the word 'entrepreneurship' could be off-putting to students, NICENT asked, not 'how to teach entrepreneurship?', but 'what do students need?' and, as a result, broadened its approach from 'enterprise for new venture creation' to 'enterprise for life' which, it believed, was more appropriate to the needs of most students and was a foundation upon which 'enterprise for new venture creation' could later be built.

There were, of course, other exceptions to the narrow 'enterprise equals start-ups' thinking. In the late 1980s in Northern Ireland the Local Enterprise Development Unit (LEDU) started to promote 'Enterprise Training' and, across the education sectors, 'Enterprise Education'. To assist in the development of its strategy for this, LEDU encouraged and/or commissioned feedback on the then current views and practice and the following extract is one of the findings of a survey, also completed in 1991, of the enterprise education element:

'All respondents highlighted the contribution that enterprise education activities in schools make to the personal and social development of young people. This was seen to be a significant reason for engaging in enterprise activities, since the Education Reform Order (NI) 1989 affirms schools' statutory responsibility to provide personal and social education as well as intellectual development.'[12]

The review in this section therefore suggests that the word 'enterprise' has often been used, more or less interchangeably with 'entrepreneurship', especially in a narrow sense to refer to the conditions which lead to business start-ups. But it has also been used in a wider sense to refer to the condition of being enterprising in any activity, not just business - and it is often not clear which use is intended. As one review found: 'the operational definitions of "enterprise" and "entrepreneurship" in HEIs vary and there are many educational aspects covered including: employability skills; social enterprise; self-employment; venture creation; employment in small businesses; [and] small business management'.[13]

Entrepreneurship: Interest and Interpretations

Possibly the hardest of the three 'E' terms to pin down is 'entrepreneurship'. The word itself appears to have been coined in the 1930s and it then started to be the subject of academic interest which has subsequently grown considerably:

'Since the first entrepreneurship course at Harvard Business School was delivered in 1947, entrepreneurship education (EE) programmes in higher education have grown rapidly and globally. This growth reflects increasing recognition that university-based EE programmes ... promise to support a range of potential entrepreneurial outcomes. For example, enhanced student venture creation skills ... business start-ups and overall job creation ultimately contributing to economic growth and development.'[14]

'Most university-level programs are intended to increase entrepreneurial awareness and to prepare aspiring entrepreneurs.' ... 'In general business planning is the primary vehicle used by the majority of courses and programs' ... [and] many universities provide entrepreneurship education with a venture creation focus.'[15]

'The purpose of the entrepreneurial awareness education is to allow students to develop entrepreneurial skills, and to assist them in choosing a career.'[16]

However, official interest in the concept labelled 'enterprise' or 'entrepreneurship' seems to have been driven mainly by economic policy concerns - in particular because it was thought that it was the condition which encouraged people to create businesses which would in turn provide jobs (for themselves and for others). Gibb, for example, highlighted this tension by pointing out that, although Schumpeter himself seemed to argue that entrepreneurship 'was a personal behavioural construct capable of being exhibited in different contexts', nevertheless 'it is frequently seen to be centrally concerned with new venture and particularly a growth oriented venture'.[17]

To encourage enterprise and/or entrepreneurship, a variety of programmes were provided to support, guide and/or help those seeking to start businesses including assistance in areas such as marketing, premises, finance, business planning and exporting. This was also sometimes supported by training courses - in the hope that support of that sort would make starting a business easier and less risky. As part of this educational establishments in many places began to introduce 'entrepreneurship' (or 'enterprise') education courses.

Although it has often not been clear precisely what sort of enterprise education was envisaged by policy advocates, in general the economic drive has been for more business start-ups (and better productivity) and it appears to have been assumed that start-up support and enterprise or entrepreneurship education would lead to that outcome. However, the available evidence does not support that assumption as the support offered has led to more start-ups[18] and a recent Enterprise Research Centre (ERC) press release reported a survey which found that 'more than 70% of Britons believe it is easy to start a business in the UK, but less [sic] than one in ten has any intention of doing so'[19]. Therefore, although it was thought that providing education and support would lead to more people becoming entrepreneurs and starting businesses, the lack of take-up could be because it is actually **intention** and not **assistance** which is the main thing missing - and intentions would appear to be influenced by social norms and preferences, not by official support programmes.

Another complication is that, as is the case with 'enterprise' and despite the early focus on business creation, different definitions of 'entrepreneurship' abound. Bridge, for example, has shown how these range from being enterprising in any situation to the creation specifically of high growth businesses. Indeed, according to a senior faculty member at Harvard Business School, the field of entrepreneurship is 'an intellectual onion. You peel it back layer by layer and when you get to the centre, there is nothing there, but you are crying.'

Even within Northern Ireland's government and its agencies this lack of consistency can be found as these two official examples illustrate:

- The Northern Ireland government's Entrepreneurship and Education Action Plan indicated that for the plan entrepreneurship was considered to be 'the ability of an individual, possessing a range of essential skills and attributes, to make a unique, innovative and creative contribution in the world of work, whether in employment or self-employment'.

- Invest Northern Ireland declared that its Accelerating Entrepreneurship Strategy 'will increasingly emphasise the acceleration of high-potential existing and start-up companies ... (to) provide the supply line for future exports based on new product and process innovation'.

To resolve this dilemma, explanations of 'entrepreneurship' have been sought which would encompass both aims and the various different definitions offered. Gartner likened this to looking for the elephant - with reference to the story of the blind men who all felt an elephant but identified what they had encountered as different things because they felt different parts of the animal. However, once the whole animal was perceived, the relationship between the parts that each had encountered could be understood. Thus, Gartner suggested, there was a drive to identify the phenomenon of which the apparently different objectives of entrepreneurship education could all be seen to be a part. But, he declared, that elephant does not exist!

'Entrepreneurship Education'

The same confusion can also be found in 'entrepreneurship (or enterprise) education'. Observers such as Brentnall *et al*, Hytti and Kuopusjärvi and Hannon all suggest that courses thus labelled can have different aims which Mitra has encompassed in his categorisation of courses as being about, for, through or with entrepreneurship - which might be summarised as:

About: Awareness of the significance and nature of enterprise and entrepreneurship and a focus on knowledge specific to new firm formation or innovation.

For: To encourage the development of new business ventures.

Through: Student-centred experimental and action learning.

With: Added-value entrepreneurship supplementing a wide range of disciplines.

Within this, a key distinction is whether the main focus should be on helping people to be more enterprising generally or on helping them to be entrepreneurs and start businesses. However, it would seem that it has often been convenient to conflate these two aims because:

- It is believed that they are more or less the same thing.
- It is customary and/or because it avoids the bother of trying to distinguish between different aims and/or adopting different approaches for them.
- The same programme can then appeal to different advocates and be 'sold' to different funders.

It has also been noted that the term 'entrepreneurship' itself can be off-putting to some people who think it has connotations of capitalism and personal greed, which are contrary to the needs of today's sustainability objectives in a world of limited resources. However, as Gibb stated:

'Many teachers were found to be hostile to the notion of teaching anything labelled "entrepreneurship" across the curriculum because of its connotations of capitalism and commercialisation. They would however see the development of the "enterprising person" as a key goal of education. Yet many of the personal attributes of such a person (creativity, initiative taking, autonomy etc) are virtually identical to those commonly associated with the entrepreneur!'

Other Considerations

As well as the different definitions and interpretations of employability, enterprise and entrepreneurship (the three 'Es') there are other factors which can affect their consideration.

A Variety of Stakeholders

Beaumont speaks of 'the various external factors at play' in this area and these include the various advocates, providers or consumers of these forms of education - such as:

- **Students.** What do (should) students want: preparation for life today, preparation for current and likely future employment options including employment, self-employment, freelance work and business creation?

- **Education providers.** Institutions want to be funded and then to make a helpful and appropriate contribution.

- **The education system.** While apparently acknowledging (some of) the value of enterprise/entrepreneurship education, official education providers do not usually assess it and, without official accreditation, it is not valued by the system or by many others either.

- **Employers.** In 2022 the All Party Parliamentary Group on Entrepreneurship published a report which concluded that UK business owners lack the core skills needed to run 'successful' and 'productive' businesses - and these core skills are 1) how to work with other people, 2) how to solve problems, 3) how to communicate effectively, 4) how to keep going in the face of challenges. However, while employers want people who will be good employees, they often lack the understanding and vocabulary to specify what that really entails?

- **Economic policy aim(s).** As explained above, a common economic policy aim is to have more small businesses and therefore for the education which will deliver that outcome. But does teaching how to start a business lead to more people doing it? Or would an encouragement to be enterprising be a better foundation for start-ups?

Three Objectives

Not least because of the different requirements of these advocates of employability, enterprise and/or entrepreneurship education, different interpretations of them have evolved. Broadly, it could be said that these programmes have one (or more) of the following three generally stated aims but, although these aims are not the same, they are not necessarily always assigned to separate delivery programmes in a clear and consistent way:

- To equip students to be more employable and more productive in employment (and thus better prepared to contribute well in existing jobs).

- To prepare students to be more enterprising (and thus better prepared to survive, advance and prosper in an uncertain world, whatever job opportunities there may be).

- To prepare students to undertake freelance work and/or start their own businesses (and thus be entrepreneurs) and to encourage them so to do.

Bridge *et al* have referred to these themes as

- employability,
- enterprise for life and
- enterprise for new venture creation

and suggested the following distinction between them. However, this categorisation is about the results of the relevant learning processes and does not indicate how they might be delivered.

'Employability
(being able to get the jobs that exist)

- Is a preparation for working for other people.
- Is being better equipped to get existing jobs - by 'selling' oneself to employers.
- Is being able to contribute in employment by having the appropriate skills and understanding that the job requires.'

'Enterprise for life
(being able to get on, even when the right job doesn't already exist)

- Is a foundation for later 'enterprise for new venture creation'.
- Supports later idea spin-out and business creation.
- Enhances employability through 'intrapreneurship' (being an entrepreneurial employee).
- Is a foundation also for social entrepreneurship.
- Is useful in subjects for which there are not enough existing jobs.
- Is an essential approach for careers in areas such as film and theatre where being able to organise a production or event is important.
- Develops the capacity to respond positively to change.'

'Enterprise for new venture creation
(being able to start a business and thus create a job)

- Assumes that the aim is new business creation.
- Has generally taught the business plan. But, although this can also help to introduce enterprise attributes and considerations (enterprise for life') it may not always be an appropriate approach even for those who do want to start a business.'

An Underlying Economic Policy Influence?

In his book *We Don't Know Ourselves,* Fintan O'Toole suggests that Ireland found a way to keep economic transformation separate from the process of indigenous organic change and, in effect, treated the idea of economic development as a separate sphere.

Has the education system similarly treated economic development considerations such as training for work or business creation, or even more general training for life, as somehow a different sphere from the main practice of 'education'?

Has the purpose of formal education been viewed as delivering the basics (the three Rs) followed by the core skills/knowledge needed for progression 'ideally' to university and then for professional employment? Has this resulted in the lack of parity in esteem between valuing 'professional employment' versus 'traditional trades' and even 'entrepreneurial small business start-up')?

The current interest in employability, enterprise and/or entrepreneurship has been encouraged by an economic development aspiration but have they then been viewed as optional add-ons to the standard education provision? Is there also a tendency, when education tries to respond to appeals to help the economy, that it focuses on those economic outputs lauded by economic policy, such as business start-ups and the skills apparently sought by inward investment businesses, rather than the more tenuous concepts of 'enterprise' and 'employability'?

On Reflection

Many views of employability, enterprise and entrepreneurship education have been advanced and this chapter has only considered a few. Even so, this sample does indicate that there are different aims and interpretations and no clear consensus on the definitions of, and distinctions between, these concepts.

Although 'employability' might seem to be the clearest, its interpretations (or the requirements for it) overlap with 'enterprise' in its broader interpretation. Indeed, 'enterprise' can be thought of as 'enterprise for life' but it also has a narrower interpretation related to business creation which is more or less the same as some interpretations of 'entrepreneurship'. And the word 'entrepreneurship' especially is a Humpty Dumpty word to which its users may attach a particular meaning but that is not necessarily the way others will understand it.

Therefore, caution is needed when dealing with this vocabulary if misunderstanding is to be avoided. In particular:

- The definitions used in practice allow for considerable overlap between the suggested categories.

- In practice some programmes, either in intention or in practice, do seem to encompass more than one of these aims - sometimes not acknowledging the difference and thus essentially treating them as the same thing.

- Others instead distinguish between entrepreneurship education as being about starting and growing a business and enterprise education as being about enabling those receiving it to be more enterprising in any aspect of life. Sometimes 'enterprise' courses are seen to be wide enough to include considerations of employability. As Beaumont observes: 'It is worth noting that ... the models often become "stuck" in the political, societal, economic, and technological space in which they were created. Consequently, they are in danger of aging, risking their current and future relevance'.

- While employability education is often seen as helping people to be more employable and better able to get the jobs created by others, some view it as being about finding some form of income generation which may, possibly by necessity, include self-employment/freelance work and thus, in effect, business start-up. Also, sometimes it is not considered to be a distinct separate category in its own silo but, in the view of many, cannot be separated from enterprise. 'I would struggle if you asked me to define the difference between employability and enterprise.'

- Sometimes employability, enterprise and entrepreneurship appear to be treated as if they are practically the same thing which can be conflated under one heading - for instance in an EU report which includes this declaration of the objectives of entrepreneurship education:

- 'Improvement of the entrepreneurial mindset of young people to enable them to be more creative and self-confident in whatever they undertake and to improve their attractiveness for employers.

- Encourage innovative business start-ups.

- Improvement of their role in society and the economy.'

Conclusion

This review of the origins and interpretations of the terms employability, enterprise and entrepreneurship indicates that there is a lack of agreement about what they are.

Are they advocated, for instance, primarily for the benefit the economy - for which both employability and preparation for business creation have been advanced as desirable outputs from the education system? Or are they advocated for the benefit of students for whom it might be advantageous to be more employable and also, generally, more enterprising, as distinct from just knowing how to start a business?

Part of the problem in discussing these topics is the lack of a clear agreed vocabulary. As indicated above, words like 'entrepreneurship' are used in different and sometime conflicting ways. Therefore, except when quoting verbatim from others, this book tries to use alternative or defined expressions for such 'slippery concepts' - for instance referring to 'enterprise for life' and 'enterprise for new venture creation' to indicate the different meanings of entrepreneurship.

Nevertheless, even with that change, this chapter has not suggested a way of viewing the three Es which both describes what each is and how they differ, and is consistent with the various observations of them in practice. Therefore, the next chapter explores a different perspective to see if it can provide a clearer and/or more useful picture.

References

1 S. Montanto, 'Developing an ecosystem: employability skills and authentic assessments', Ch11 in Hansen S. L. and Daniels K. (editors), How to Enable the Employability of University Graduates, (Cheltenham: Edward Elgar, 2023)

2 E. Beaumont, '"One for all and all for one": the 3Es (employability, enterprise, and entrepreneurship)' Ch18 in Hansen S. L. and Daniels K. (editors), How to Enable the Employability of University Graduates, (Cheltenham: Edward Elgar, 2023)

3 S. L. Hansen and K. Daniels (editors), How to Enable the Employability of University Graduates, (Cheltenham: Edward Elgar, 2023

4 M. Yorke, Employability in Higher Education: What is it - what is it not?, (York: The Higher Education Academy, 2006)

5 CBI (Confederation of British Industry), Making Employability Work: An Agenda for Action, (London: CBI, 1999)

6 M. Cheng, O. Adekola, J. Albia and S. Cai, 'Employability in Higher Education: a review of key stakeholders' perspectives', Higher Education Evaluation and Development, Vol.16 No.1, 2021, pp.16-31

7 G. Mason, G. Williams and S. Cranmer, 'Employability skills initiatives in higher education: what effects do they have on graduate labour market outcomes?', Education Economics, Vol.17 No.1, 2009, pp.1-30

8 3E podcasts, www.advance-he.ac.uk/knowledge-hub/3e-podcast (accessed 3 October 2023)

9 See, for example, S. Bridge and K. O'Neill, Understanding Enterprise, Entrepreneurs and small Business, London: Palgrave, 2018) p.19/20

10 'Towards an "Enterprising" Culture - A Challenge for Education and Training', OECD/CERI Educational Monograph, No. 4 (1989) pp. 6-7.

11 S. Bridge, C. Hegarty and S. Porter, 'Rediscovering Enterprise: Developing Appropriate University Entrepreneurship Education', Education + Training, Vol.52 No.8/9, 2010, pp.722-734

12 ITS and Mentor, (1991), Enterprise Education in Northern Ireland, (Report commissioned by LEDU, August 1991)

13 L. Pittaway and J. Cope, 'Entrepreneurship Education: A Systematic Review of the Evidence', International Small Business Journal, Vol.25 No.5, 2007, p.480

14 G. Nabi, F. Liňán, A. Fayolle, N. Krueger and A. Walmsley, 'The Impact of Entrepreneurship Education in Higher Education: A Systematic Review and Research Agenda', Academy of Management Learning & Education, Vol.16 No.2, 2017, pp.277-299

15 T. J. Bae, S. Qian, C. Miao and J. O. Fiet, 'The relationship between Entrepreneurship Education and Entrepreneurial Intentions: A Meta-Analytic Review', Entrepreneurship Theory and Practice, Vol.38 No.2, 2014, pp.217-254

16 F. Liňán quoted by T. J. Bae, S. Qian, C. Miao and J. O, Fiet, 'The relationship between Entrepreneurship Education and Entrepreneurial Intentions: A Meta-Analytic Review', Entrepreneurship Theory and Practice, Vol.38 No.2, 2014, p.219

17 A. A. Gibb, 'Concepts into practice: meeting the challenge of development of entrepreneurship educators around an innovative paradigm', International Journal of Entrepreneurial Behaviour & Research, Vol.17 No.2, 2011, p.150

18 See Chapter 16 of S. Bridge and K. O'Neill, Understanding Enterprise, Entrepreneurs and Small Business, (London: Palgrave, 2018)

19 Enterprise Research Centre, Press release, 10 Feb 2022

20 S. Bridge, Rethinking Enterprise Policy: Can Failure Trigger New Understanding, (Basingstoke: Palgrave, 2010) p.107

21 Reported in H. H. Stevenson 'Intellectual Foundations of Entrepreneurship' in Entrepreneurship: The Way Ahead, Edited by H. P. Welsch (New York and London: Routledge, 2004) p. 3

22 The Entrepreneurship and Education Action Plan, published in March 2003, a joint plan developed by the Department of Enterprise Trade, and Investment (DETI, the Department of Education (DE) and the Department for Employment and Learning (DEL)

23 Invest Northern Ireland, Corporate Plan 2008-2011, (www.investmi.com accessed 11 February 2009) p.5

24 W. B. Gartner, 'Is there an Elephant in Entrepreneurship? Blind Assumptions in Theory Development', Entrepreneurship Theory and Practice, Vol.25 No.4, 2001, pp.27-39

25 C. Brentnall, I. D Rodriguez. and N. Culkin, 'The contribution of realist evaluation to critical analysis of the effectiveness of entrepreneurship education competitions', Industry and Higher Education, Vol.32 No.6, 2018, pp.405-417

26 U. Hytti and P. Kuopusjärvi, 'Three Perspectives to Evaluating Entrepreneurship Education: Evaluators, Programme Promoters and Policy Makers', paper presented at the efmd 34th EISB Conference, Turku 2004, based on Evaluating and Measuring Entrepreneurship and Enterprise Education, Small Business Institute, Turku, Finland, 2004 - from a Leonardo funded project.

26 P. Hannon, 'Philosophies of Enterprise and Entrepreneurship Education and the Challenges for Higher Education in the UK', International Journal of Entrepreneurship and Innovation, Vol.6 No.2, 2005, pp.105-114

27 J. Mitra, 'Holistic experimentation for emergence: A creative approach to postgraduate entrepreneurship education and training', Industry and Higher Education, Vol.31 No.1, 2016, pp.34-50

28 S. Bridge, C. Hegarty and S. Porter, 'Rediscovering enterprise: delivering appropriate university entrepreneurship education, Education + Training, Vol.52 No.8/9, 2010, pp.722-7,34

29 A. A. Gibb, 'Concepts into practice: meeting the challenge of development of entrepreneurship educators around an innovative paradigm', International Journal of Entrepreneurial Behaviour & Research, Vol.17 No.2, 2011, p.151

31 E. Beaumont, '"One for all and all for one": the 3Es (employability, enterprise, and entrepreneurship)' Ch18 in S. L Hansen. and K. Daniels (editors), How to Enable the Employability of University Graduates, (Cheltenham: Edward Elgar, 2023)

32 J. Lockyer, 'Educate, Innovate, Empower', ISBE Policy and Practice Insights, Vol.1 Issue 2, 2023

33 S. Bridge, C. Hegarty and S. Porter, 'Rediscovering enterprise: delivering appropriate university entrepreneurship education, Education + Training, Vol.52 No.8/9, 2010, pp.722-7,34

34 F. O'Toole, We Don't Know Ourselves, (London: Head of Zeus Ltd, 2021) p.564

35 Lewis Carroll, Through the Looking Glass

36 E. Beaumont, '"One for all and all for one": the 3Es (employability, enterprise, and entrepreneurship)' Ch18 in Hansen S. L. and Daniels K. (editors), (2023), How to Enable the Employability of University Graduates, (Cheltenham: Edward Elgar, 2023)

37 3E podcasts, www.advance-he.ac.uk/knowledge-hub/3e-podcast (accessed 3 October 2023)

38 EU, Effects and impact of entrepreneurship programmes in higher education, (Brussels: EU Directorate General for Enterprise and Industry, March 2012) p.7

CHAPTER 3

ECONOMIC EDUCATION: A COMMON SET OF COMPONENTS

Chapter Summary

Chapter 2 points out, not only that one of the purposes of education has been identified as economic, but also that there has been a growing advocacy for education specifically for employability, enterprise and entrepreneurship. However, while employability, enterprise and entrepreneurship are often spoken of together, they are usually viewed as being separate but they lack clear accepted descriptions.

Attempts to unite them by looking above them for an overall unifying concept have failed and this chapter suggests that this perspective would work better in reverse by looking under the three labels and examining the attributes of which they appear to be formed. Instead of being different components of the same thing, the things viewed do appear instead to be different constructs supported and enabled by a common set of core skills and abilities. This may not have been immediately obvious because those components have been given a variety of different labels and also grouped together in different ways. Nevertheless, when they are examined and compared, as is attempted in this chapter, the similarities become more apparent. However, as in many developments of knowledge and understanding, it takes time for old ways of thinking to be abandoned and new perspectives to be adopted.

The common set of components from which employability, enterprise or entrepreneurship might be developed are sometime labelled 'transversal' (with a few specific additions in some cases). Further the list of components thus indicated appears to have a lot in common with advocated sets of life competencies - which adds to the case for including them in the education provision.

Introduction

Chapter 2 points out, not only that one of the purposes of education has been identified as economic, but also that there has been a growing advocacy specifically for employability, enterprise and entrepreneurship education.

However, while those three concepts are often spoken of together, they are usually viewed as being separate although they lack clear and widely agreed descriptions or definitions, especially in the case of 'entrepreneurship' which has been defined in a variety of different ways.

To try to resolve this, as also noted in Chapter 2, attempts have been made to reconcile the apparently different interpretations, particularly of 'entrepreneurship', by looking above them for an overarching concept of which each could be seen to be a part and which would explain their relationship to each other. However, as Gartner declared, that 'elephant' does not exist.[1]

Instead of looking from above for an overall linking theory, this chapter suggests that the perspective would work better in reverse by looking under the three labels and examining the components, abilities, attributes and/or skills upon which they each appear to be based. Instead of being different components of the same thing, could it be that the things viewed, the three Es, are different constructs from the same basic components? In other words, could the qualities variously labelled as employability, enterprise or entrepreneurship, and therefore the outcomes of being 'employable, being enterprising and/or starting a business, all be supported by a common set of skills (sometimes with a few specific additions)?

Instead of starting with an assumption of difference, this chapter looks at where there might be similarities: at what has been identified as the components advocated for these forms of education. It examines a selection of different commentaries and lists of the qualities, abilities, attributes and/or competencies variously ascribed to them to see whether they help to make the difference clear or if, instead, at the component level there is a lot they have in common.

Some Sample Lists

There is a variety of lists of the necessary qualities, some of which are considered here:

Enterprise Qualities

An early example of a list of enterprise qualities comes from the late 1980s when LEDU (the Northern Ireland Government's Local Enterprise Development Unit) started to promote 'enterprise training' and, in the primary, secondary and further education sectors, 'enterprise education'. To assist in the development of its strategy for this, LEDU commissioned feedback on the then views and practice and this extract is from a survey[2], completed in 1991 (and also mentioned in Chapter 2), of the enterprise education element:

Respondents commented that personal and social development is intrinsic to the whole educational process and demonstrated that enterprising activities help encourage qualities such as:

- Independence
- Self-reliance
- Problem-solving
- Self-confidence
- Communication
- Sense of "can do"
- Initiative
- Innovation and creativity
- Decision-making
- Management skills
- Taking responsibility
- Co-operation and team-working
- Leadership
- Negotiating
- Assertiveness
- Resource investigation
- Learning from mistakes
- Self-determination

Embedding Employability

In their contribution to a series intended for staff in higher education institutions who are addressing student employability, Yorke and Knight consider the background to the employability agenda and how it might be captured in the curriculum. They adopt as a working definition of employability the description that it is 'a set of achievements - skills, understandings and personal attributes - that make graduates more likely to gain employment and be successful in their chosen occupations, which benefits themselves, the workforce, the community and the economy'[3].

As well as exploring other aspects of embedding employability in an education curriculum, Yorke and Knight offer the following list of the personal qualities, core skills and process skills needed:

Personal Qualities: Malleable self-theory [i.e. a growth mindset], self-awareness, self-confidence, independence, emotional intelligence, adaptability, stress tolerance, initiative, willingness to learn, reflectiveness.

Core Skills: Reading effectiveness, numeracy, information retrieval, language skills, self-management, critical analysis, creativity: ability to be original or inventive and to apply lateral thinking, listening, written communication, oral presentations, explaining, global awareness.

Process Skills: Computer literacy, commercial awareness, political sensitivity, ability to work cross-culturally, ethical sensitivity, prioritising, planning, setting of achievable goals and structuring action, applying subject understanding, acting morally, coping with complexity, problem-solving, influencing, arguing for and/or justifying a point of view or a course of action, resolving conflict, decision making, negotiating, teamwork.

Enterprise Behaviours, Attributes and Competencies

The UK Quality Assurance Agency for Higher Education (QAA), in its guidance for enterprise and entrepreneurship education, distinguishes between enterprise education and entrepreneurship education but also refers to 'entrepreneurial' education as a 'catch all' term encompassing both. However, when considering enterprise education, it identifies the following components and suggests, not only that these can enhance employability prospects but also that entrepreneurship education can build on the indicated enterprising competencies:

'*Enterprise behaviours* [which] can include taking the initiative, making things happen, reflecting, communicating, pivoting and adapting, storytelling, taking responsibility, networking, personal effectiveness and managed risk taking.'

'*Enterprise attributes* [which] can include open mindedness, proactivity, curiosity, self-efficacy, flexibility, adaptability, determination and resilience.'

'*Enterprise competencies* [which] can include intuitive decision making, identifying opportunities, creative problem solving, innovating, strategic thinking, design thinking, negotiation, communicating, influencing, leadership and financial, business and digital literacy.'[4]

Conflating Employability and Enterprise

The QAA guidance is not the only source linking the components of employability and enterprise. Dean has noted that, back in 1992, Watts and Hawthorn had provided definitions of 'enterprise' that could subsume the concept of employability. Therefore, in 2010, she wondered if they could be conflated and produced a diagram which listed the following skills required for both agendas[5]:

Employability Skills: Working within systems, Teamwork, Career management

Common Skills. Communication, Problem-solving, Spotting opportunities, Initiative, Creativity, Flexibility Self-awareness, Decision-making, Networking

Enterprise Skills. Creating opportunities, Creating new systems, Financial Management

Entrepreneurship Competencies

A list of competencies specifically for entrepreneurship has been provided by the European Commission. It has developed EntreComp: the European Entrepreneurship Competence Framework as a reference framework to explain what is mean by an entrepreneurial mindset and a guide to the knowledge, skills and attitudes that people need to be entrepreneurial and create financial, cultural or social value for others. For this, EntreComp identifies 15 competencies in three key areas[6]:

Ideas and Opportunities: Spotting opportunities, creativity, vision, valuing ideas, ethical and sustainable thinking.

Resources: Self-awareness and self-efficiency, motivation and perseverance, mobilising resources, financial and economic literacy, mobilising others.

Into Action: Taking the initiative, planning and management, coping with uncertainty, ambiguity and risk, working with others, learning through experience

Wider Core Competencies

Although the lists considered above have been specifically suggested for economic application, it is clear that they have a lot in common with wider lists - such as the following:

A University Objective

The University of the West of Scotland (UWS) has as its objective 'to develop graduates who are universal, work-ready and successful'[7] and for this it has identified a number of academic, personal and professional attributes to be developed including:

Academic: critical thinker, analytical, inquiring, knowledgeable, digitally literate, problem solver, autonomous, incisive, innovative

Personal: emotionally intelligent, ethically minded, culturally aware, effective communicator, influential, motivated, creative, imaginative, resilient

Professional: collaborative, research minded, socially responsible, potential leader, enterprising, ambitious, driven, daring, transformational

A Core Competency List

For example, as reported in Chapter 1, Sir Ken Robinson suggests that the purposes of education are personal, cultural, economic and social. With this somewhat wider perspective he asks what students should know and be able to do as a result of their education and, he suggests that they should be equipped to engage in the personal, cultural, economic, and social challenges they will inevitably face in their lives. Then, for this, he suggests that the following eight core competencies will be needed[8]:

'Curiosity - the ability to ask questions and explore how the world works.

Creativity - the ability to generate new ideas and to apply them in practice.

Criticism - the ability to analyse information and ideas and to form reasoned arguments and judgements.

Communication - the ability to express thoughts and feelings clearly and confidently in a range of media and forms.

Collaboration - the ability to work constructively with others.

Compassion - the ability to empathise with others and act accordingly.

Composure - the ability to connect with the inner life of feeling and develop a sense of personal harmony and balance.

Citizenship - the ability to engage constructively with society and to participate in the processes that sustain it.'

A Synthesis

Trying to identify and then list all the skills, attributes and/or competencies not just in the lists mentioned above but others also, is not an easy task. Even on a quick count it is possible to identify over 100 labels just from the lists mentioned.

However, these labels do not all refer to clearly distinct individual skills. Instead, some of them are better understood as referring to domains of skill and, in any case, those domains and skills are not clearly bounded and separate but overlap with, or shade into, others.

Another feature of many of the relevant skills is that they are not limited in application to one specific task but are transferable to a range of different situations. Therefore, attempts have been made to identify categories of skill which are necessary for successful endeavour in different situations - such as transversal and uber skills:

Transversal skills
In contrast to listing components suggested specifically for employability, enterprise and/or entrepreneurship, UNESCO[9] has listed transversal skills which, it suggests, are 'skills that are typically considered as not specifically related to a particular job, task, academic discipline or area of knowledge and that can be used in a wide variety of situations and work settings' and suggests five categories of such skills:

'Critical and innovative thinking. Inter-personal skills (e.g. presentation and communication skills, organisational skills, teamwork etc).

Intra-personal skills (e.g. self-discipline, enthusiasm, perseverance, self-motivation etc).

Global citizenship (e.g. tolerance, openness, respect for diversity, intercultural understanding etc).

Media and information literacy - such as the ability to locate and access information, as well as to analyse and evaluate media content.'

Uber skills
In a similar vein Skills Development Scotland[10] has identified a set of 'innate, timeless, higher-order skills that create adaptive learners able to succeed whatever the future brings'. Others have labelled these as 'meta' or 'uber' skills - and they include:

'Self-management - focus, integrity, adaptability and initiative

Social intelligence - communication, feeling, collaboration and leadership

Innovation - curiosity, sense-making, creativity and critical thinking'.

Instead of suggesting that different groups of skill are needed for specific applications, such as being employable, being enterprising or starting a new venture, these lists suggest domains of skill which would support all such endeavours. A possible analogy for this is that, instead of providing separate Lego kits for each three different toy cars, a common set of Lego components could be assembled from which any of the cars, or other models, could be constructed, albeit possibly with a few special extras in some cases. For instance, if the word 'entrepreneurship' is taken to refer specifically to business creation, then, in addition to a common skills base, that might additionally require some specific start-up input.

It is therefore concluded that, instead of pursuing separate education channels for employability, enterprise or entrepreneurship, it would be helpful to try to deliver the components which would support the development of any of them - and which would help people to be better prepared for life generally. Consequently, it is suggested that the components required could be grouped into two sets:

- A general set of the skill domains needed to be more enterprising and thus better prepared for life as well as being more employable and more ready to create one's own employment if that seems to be preferable.

- The specific requirements needed for particular activities such as, for example, starting a business (see Chapter 4).

As a starting point, the following is a suggested general set of skill sets based on the above analysis and the recent experience of South Eastern Regional College (SERC):

Citizenship skills - including working cross-culturally, acting morally, tolerance and openness.

Skills for coping with uncertainty - including understanding risk and complexity and being mentally prepared to face the unexpected.

Critical thinking and creativity skills - including, creativity, generating ideas, innovation and spotting opportunities. Digital literacy skills - including media and information literacy, using ICT and AI awareness.

Skills for problem solving and decision making - including problem analysis, generating solutions and selecting the best option.

Self-management skills - including self-initiative, confidence, resilience and time management.

Work professionalism skills - including co-operation, evaluation, resolving conflict and behaving appropriately.

Skills for working with others - including communication (spoken and written), empathy, emotional intelligence and teamwork.

It is suggested that, with these skills, students should be:

- Equipped to be more employable and more productive in employment (and thus better prepared to contribute well in existing jobs).

- Prepared to be more enterprising (and thus better able to survive, advance and prosper in an uncertain world whatever job opportunities there may be).

- Prepared to undertake freelance work and/or start their own businesses (and thus be entrepreneurs) - and encouraged to do so.

Conclusion

Trying to identify clear and consistent distinctions between employability, enterprise and 'entrepreneurship' is not helpful as in common usage those terms have a variety of sometimes overlapping and sometimes conflicting meanings. However, what they do all have is a common foundation on a range of transferable skills which are helpful for all of them.

Therefore, instead of trying to devise different education courses for each one, it is suggested that they will all be supported by helping people to develop a range of transferable (transversal and uber) skill domains such as those suggested. This will also be helpful for people who may at different stages in their careers wish to switch between being employed, being enterprising and creating or running an organisation or business.

References

1 W. B. Gartner, 'Is there an Elephant in Entrepreneurship? Blind Assumptions in Theory Development', Entrepreneurship Theory and Practice, Vol.25 No.4, 2001, pp.27-39

2 ITS and Mentor, (1991), Enterprise Education in Northern Ireland, (Report commissioned by LEDU, August 1991)

3 M. Yorke and P. T. Knight, Learning and Employability: Embedding Employability into the Curriculum, (York: The Higher Education Academy, 2006)

4. QAA, Enterprise and entrepreneurship education: Guidance for UK higher education providers (Quality Assurance Agency for Higher Education, 2018, January). p.9 https://www.qaa.ac.uk/docs/qaa/about-us/enterprise-and-entrpreneurship-education-2018.pdf?sfvrsn=20e2f581_14 (accessed 28 October 2023)

5 L. Dean, 'Enterprise and employability: to conflate or not to conflate', (Leeds Metropolitan University: Assessment, Teaching and Learning Journal No.8, Spring 2010, pp.21-23

6 EntreComp into Action User Guide 2018, https://publications.jrc.ec.europa.eu/repository/handle/JRC109128 (accessed 8 Oct 2023)

7 A. Murray and R. J. Crammond, 'Witnessing entrepreneurial perceptions and proclivity in university students', Education + Training, Vol.62 No.4, 2020, pp.459-481

8 Sir Ken Robinson and K. Robinson, Imagine If..., (London: Penguin, 2022) pp.44-50

9 See for instance UNESCO, Education Policy Brief (Vol.2), 2014: Skills for holistic human development, https://unesdoc.unesco.org/ark:/48223/pf0000245064/PDF/245064eng.pdf.multi (accessed 9 Oct 2023)

10 Skills Development Scotland, A guide to meta-skills across the curriculum, September 2021 (www.skills developmentscotland.co.uk accessed 16 May 2024)

CHAPTER 4

START-UP: AN EXCEPTION

Chapter Summary

Employability, enterprise and entrepreneurship are based on a common set of skills (abilities, attributes and/or competencies). However, the process of starting a business also requires a number of other specific inputs. Therefore, if entrepreneurship is taken to refer to, or to include, the process of new venture creation, additional knowledge and knowhow will be helpful. This chapter considers start-up conditions and process and the occasional need for specific guidance about it.

Introduction

Chapters 2 and 3 have looked at 'employability', enterprise' and 'entrepreneurship' education and Chapter 3 suggests that there is common a set of skills which are the foundation that people need to be employable, to be enterprising or to be entrepreneurs and start businesses.

However, it also notes that, while the process of actually starting a business does require those skills, it also needs several particular business inputs. For instance, not only is some specific knowhow about the business process necessary but the Enterprise Research Centre (ERC) press release quoted in Chapter 2 indicates, at least in the UK, many people also need appropriate motivation if they are to start a business.

In many places, economic policy considerations and especially a desire to increase the business start-up rate has led to official support including specifically 'entrepreneurship education' in the apparent expectation that it will have such an effect. Therefore, for those who wish to focus on 'entrepreneurship' interpreted in this way as 'enterprise for new venture creation', this chapter looks at these specific requirements and considers how many of them might be supplied by an educational environment.

The Ingredients for Start-up Courses

Despite the variety of enterprise or entrepreneurship courses purporting to encourage business start-up, it would seem that there is no clear generally accepted syllabus for this to replace the once favoured practice of basing teaching on the common business plan format. That would often cover the types of things which a sustainable business might be expected to show: such as a summary of the business idea, an analysis of the prospective market, a sales forecast, a description of the production process and the initial investment needed and viable financial projections based on this.

However, in some quarters start-up business plans are now being criticised. They have been described as being 'just like a road map and the planning process is just like map-reading'[1] - but how can you have a reliable map for the future which is as yet unexplored and un-mapped? For instance over 30 years ago, when business plans started to become advocated as the tool to help start-ups, a business professor observed to one of the authors that she and two colleagues had started a consulting business but it was not until they had had three years of operating experience that they actually had the information they needed to write such a plan.

Despite this, through a process of copying the apparent custom and practice of others, the business plan often appears to be accepted as the appropriate foundation for approaching the process of starting a business. Its use has therefore become the conventional wisdom - but there are contrary views, such as this by an entrepreneurship educator:

We have all heard the growing chorus ... debating the proper role, if any, for teaching business plans. A valid criticism ... is that the way business plans have been traditionally taught results in well-written "works of fiction".'[2]

That is one of many voices now being raised against the business plan as the key tool for business start-up[3], not least because this approach appears to advocate researching and forecasting to provide appropriate base for planning - instead of learning how to operate in conditions of uncertainty. As Mintzberg put it:

'As we enter this discussion ... it would be well to bear in mind the disarmingly simple point that "the future does not exist; how could there be knowledge about something non-existent"?'[4].

Of course, a business plan can have its uses - for instance if a prospective funder asks to see it. Therefore, as Sarasvathy advocates in presenting her ideas for an 'effectual' approach[5], have both tools in your toolbox. But the limitations of business plans are gaining more recognition and it is becoming more widely accepted that they are not the apparently essential all-purpose tool for start-up as they appear sometimes to be presented.

There is no clear widely agreed replacement and, therefore, instead of continuing to look for a definitive list of start-up needs, this chapter presents its own suggestion (see 4.1).

4.1 - The Requirements for Starting a New Business

What are the requirements, the things that need to be done or in place, if someone is to start a new business? The following list is offered as a starting point:

Motivation
People are unlikely to want to start a business without being motivated so to do (and perceived social disapproval might even prevent further consideration). That motivation could come from one or more of several sources / reasons, including:

Peer example and encouragement from a social environment which sees starting a business as an acceptable and even admirable activity.

A need (and no better alternative for addressing it) such as for:

- Money.
- Independence and being one's own boss.
- Achievement and leaving a legacy.
- To practice a skill.
- Social acceptability.

Self-belief when encountering an opportunity and not being conditioned to 'fear failure'.

Idea

Starting a business requires an idea for a product or service which the business could provide and someone is likely to buy.

Mindset

To start a business it helps to have a growth mindset rather than a fixed one. With a growth mindset people believe their abilities and talents can be developed through passion, education and persistence, whereas with a fixed mindset they believe their talents and abilities are fixed and nothing can be done to change them.

Abilities and skills

Starting a business is likely to be easier if the person (or people) doing it has appropriate abilities and skills - including:

- Being enterprising and innovative.
- Being prepared to face uncertainty, to explore and to apply 'trial and error' - but not to ignore risk.
- Being able to spot opportunity.

Awareness of methods

Awareness of methods, techniques or 'tools' which are available to guide or assist the process of starting a business, and knowing how and when to apply them, could be helpful. These might include effectuation, lean start-up, design thinking, ready-fire-aim and even sometimes the business plan.

Process understanding

Knowing what is required for the process - which can include:

- The necessary bureaucratic steps for setting up a business.
- The legal requirements - e.g. for registration, taxation (including VAT), employment etc.

Business skills

Running a business requires the application of skills/abilities including specifically the following (but these are unlikely all to be possessed by a single individual - so help from associates, partners, employees, and/or friends etc may be needed).

- Market skills - market analysis and the ability to sell.
- Financial management.
- People management (if there are any employees).
- The ability to produce the product or service to be offered.

Resources

Starting a business is a bit like flying a glider which needs help to get launched but then, once aloft and if piloted with sufficient skill, should be able to find enough lift to sustain its flight. The sort of things a business needs at the start include:

- Financial capital - but an 'effectuation' (affordable loss) approach can help.
- Other business requirements - such as premises, raw materials/supplies, customers, and employees.
- Social capital - an often-overlooked resource which can provide or help to build/acquire things like information, trust and mutual obligations, and norms and reinforcement.

This list tries to consider all the requirements for someone to start a business with a reasonable prospect of success, not just the ones that might usually be taught in a start-up course. It shows however that there are things that could be taught beyond the component skills suggested in Chapter 3 - such as business skills and an understanding of the start-up requirements and process. Therefore, those components could be supplemented by a specific start-up course.

However, the list also suggests that such a course alone would not be enough to persuade more people to start businesses. As Decker-Lange *et al* note: 'We still have a way to go in this country for entrepreneurship to be seen as a normal and desirable graduate outcome'[6] .Therefore, as well as education, starting a business would also need things like more positive influencer encouragement plus access to the necessary resources. Nevertheless, a course could help to present the start-up option in a positive light and might include signposting to other possible sources of help.

The Requisite Capitals

If entrepreneurship is assumed to mean business start-up, then the actual process of starting a business would not be well covered just by the suggested set of employability/enterprise skill components.

Therefore, if promoting start-up is the aim, a special extra provision should be made. For instance, it could be said to require human, intellectual, physical, financial and social capital.

However, while guidance in the start-up process and training in the necessary skills (sometimes referred to as the 'human capital') might be provided in a dedicated education provision, the suggested list of the requirements needed for someone to start a business includes many things that are beyond what an education course might provide. It requires an idea and an understanding of how to realise it (intellectual capital), facilities and raw material (physical capital), and money (financial capital). And, often overlooked, it needs, or will be assisted by, motivation, encouragement, moral support and supportive contacts, all of which can be classed as 'social capital'.

Therefore, just providing 'entrepreneurship education' and financial support is unlikely itself to lead to more start-ups because what is also needed for that is the motivation and social support to do it.

References

1 Burns P., Entrepreneurship and Small Business (3rd Edition), (Basingstoke: Palgrave, 2011) p.365

2 J. Cornwall, The Entrepreneurship Educator Newsletter, June 2010

2 See, for instance Chapter 3 of S. Bridge and C. Hegarty, Beyond the Business Plan: 10 principles for new venture explorers, (Basingstoke: Palgrave Macmillan, 2013)

4 Mintzberg H., The Rise and Fall of Strategic Planning, (Hemel Hempstead: Prentice Hall, 1994) p.229

5 S. Sarasvathy, Effectuation: Elements of Entrepreneurial Experience, (Cheltenham: Edward Elgar, 2008)

6 C. Decker-Lange, K. Lange and A. Walmsley, 'How does entrepreneurship education affect employability? Insights from UK higher education', International Journal of Entrepreneurial Behaviour & Research. EarlyCite Accepted Feb 2024

CHAPTER 5

TRANSVERSAL SKILLS - AND THEIR PLACE IN EDUCATION

Chapter Summary

Chapter 3 concluded that the economic applications of employability, enterprise and entrepreneurship are all supported by a common set of skills which are required, not just for economic activity, but for making the most of many life opportunities.

These have been referred to as transversal or T skills and they are mainly acquired, not through knowledge acquisition like many school subjects, but by guided practice. And they are relevant, not just for the world of work, but many other aspects of life.

It is suggested that, to see how would these fit into the education system, four categories of education provision should be recognised:

- The basics such as the traditional foundation of the three Rs - which could be termed R proficiencies.
- Then the standard classroom subjects often taught in silos - or S learning.
- At all levels there are then relevant transversal abilities - or T skills.
- And also unifying higher level (uber) skills - or U skills.

This R-S-T-U classification provides a framework and vocabulary for describing and positioning the different aspects of education needed for life and success in the 21stcentury. It could help to show how the different skill categories relate to each other and what might be missing in a particular application. Also, to promote recognition, consideration and adoptions of T and U skills, a suggested vocabulary is offered for them. Examples of how they can be developed and assessed are then provided in Part II.

Introduction

Chapter 3 showed that the economic applications of employability, enterprise and entrepreneurship are all supported by a common set of skills (also sometimes labelled abilities and/or competencies) which enable, not only economic activity, but also many other life opportunities. Therefore, they could be said to be a key part of the link between formal education and a thriving society.

As well as the obviously economically focussed sources noted in Chapter 3, there are many other observations which also support this suggestion that skills such as these are an important part of life preparation:

- The OECD Learning Compass talks of 'transformative competencies' which it defines as 'the types of knowledge, skills, attitudes and values students need to transform society and shape the future for better lives'[1]. The Learning Compass 2030 is composed of seven elements: core foundations, transformative competencies, student agency and co-agency, knowledge (disciplinary, interdisciplinary, epistemic and procedural), skills (cognitive and metacognitive; social and emotional; and practical and physical), attitudes and values, and the anticipation-action-reflection cycle.

- AEGEE (Association des Etats Généraux des Etudiants de l'Europe) suggests that in a modern Europe young people need transversal skills and competences which are 'the skills, knowledge and attitudes relevant to a broad range of occupations and sectors' and they are 'also defined as the basic, essential, cross-thematic, cross-curricular or 21st century skills and competences'[2]. It indicates, for example, different lists of competencies for lifelong learning, for the school to work transition and for international careers.

- UNESCO (see also in Chapter 3) lists six categories of transversal skills 'that are typically considered as not specifically related to a particular job, task, academic discipline or area of knowledge and that can be used in a wide variety of situations and work settings'[3]. These, it suggests, might also be called 'soft' or 'transferrable', because they are not specific to a particular sector or job role. The term 'transversal' refers to the way these skills 'cut across' different tasks and roles, just like a transversal line in geometry. Its suggested categories are critical and innovative thinking, interpersonal skills, intrapersonal skills, global citizenship, media and information literacy and others.

- The Cambridge Life Competencies framework specifically acknowledges that 'our world is changing fast and we need to prepare our students with the skills and experiences that go beyond learning an additional language'[4] .Therefore, to support teachers in preparing students with a positive mindset, it advocates the following competencies:

‘**Creative Thinking:** Preparing for creativity, generating ideas, and implementing ideas and solving problems

Critical Thinking: Understanding and analysing ideas and arguments, evaluating ideas and arguments and solving problems and making decisions

Learning To Learn: Developing skills and strategies for learning, taking control of own learning and reflecting on, and evaluating own learning

Communication: Using appropriate language and register for context, facilitating interactions, and participating with appropriate confidence and clarity

Collaboration: Taking personal responsibility for own contribution to a group task, encouraging effective group interaction, managing the sharing of tasks in a group activity, and working towards task completion

Social Responsibilities: Understanding personal responsibilities as part of a social group, showing intercultural awareness, and understanding global issues.’[5]

Imparting Transversal Skills

The skills advocated by these authorities and others are founded on ability in actually doing something rather than on the acquisition of knowledge about it.

Often, when these skills are developed, that is not through deliberate development, but unconsciously through social contact and lived experience.

However, that does not necessarily work either automatically or well for everyone - which is why such skills need to be included deliberately in the education provision. Because they are not based on knowledge absorbed, they cannot be taught through classroom instruction, which is the method for much traditional education, but can instead be acquired through tutored experience. Thus learning them is rather like learning to play a sport which many schools do teach, although not in classrooms but by coaching students while they are actually practicing the sport in question.

Therefore, to develop them, what has been termed experiential learning is appropriate. Project based learning (PBL) is an example of this method that does not focus on memorization of facts or theories but instead involves a dynamic approach in which students acquire a deeper knowledge through active exploration of real projects involving problems and challenges. Students learn about a subject by working on it for an extended period while being appropriately guided and coached to help them to direct and improve their efforts.

The Need for Assessment

This analysis has highlighted the importance of recognising that transversal skills are relevant to many aspects of life, including economic applications. However, not only are they unlike traditional school subjects in the way they have to be taught, but also they cannot be assessed by examinations testing for retained knowledge. Consequently, because they have not been included in traditional records of ability, such as exam passes, and consequently do not easily feature on CVs, they have not been given the recognition or value they merit.

Delivering Transversal Skills in Practice

Nevertheless, following recommendations such as those above, some educational establishments have started to include such skills in their educational provision. For example, in Northern Ireland, based on recommendations in particular those from UNESCO, the South Eastern Regional College (SERC) has introduced a transversal skills framework into its further education provision - and this is explained further in Part II. Its chapters describe not only the way SERC has introduced a set of skills through PBL but also how it then assesses the skills students have acquired to give them a record which can be shown to other interested parties such as prospective employers.

Relating Transversal Skills to Traditional Education

But, before that example is presented, a perspective is suggested for seeing how transversal and uber (T and U) skills align with the traditional components of education.

It is proposed that, to help to explain the situation, different categories of learning should be recognised within education - and 'mapping' this could both indicate what might be missing and show where a variety of skills would fit into the system. To do this, a categorisation of the components of education into different sorts of skills is suggested:

Foundation proficiency

- Traditional education could be summarised as covering first, at primary level, the basic foundations needed for learning including, for example, proficiency in reading, writing and arithmetic - and sometimes, if these are not well absorbed, they need to be reinforced at later stages. Together these foundations have been known as the three Rs. So this category of skills might be termed 'R' proficiencies.

Subject learning

- Then, at secondary and subsequent levels, various knowledge–based subjects are taught. Often, at secondary level this is with the aspiration that students will learn enough about these subjects to pass exams in them and thus provide them with the requirements for university entry or trade skill training. These subjects, such as the use of English, mathematics, history, geography, physics, chemistry and biology, are often studied in separate silos - so acquiring knowledge about them could be termed S learning.

Transversal skills

- However, as described above, there are also the skills needed to link S learning about different subjects and to equip students to apply their learning in the activities of their lives - and these have been described as soft skills or transversal skills and could thus be labelled T skills.

Uber skills

- Finally, there could be considered to be another level of skill, such as leadership and managing meetings, which might not be needed by everyone. These could be considered to be higher (or uber) skills which might therefore be termed U skills.

While there is, and has been, a clear need for R proficiency as a base for progressing to S learning, T skills are not a further progression from S learning as there is a need for T skills at every level of learning and later life. Even at primary level some T skills are required such as being able to express oneself and to relate to others. Such skills are often acquired naturally through social interaction but were sometimes found to be lacking in young children after the Covid pandemic when face-to-face gatherings had been suspended. U skills, however, may not be needed at early stages but can usefully start to be acquired at secondary level.

Figure 5.1 –A 'Map' of the Categories of Possible Education Provision– with example skills and shading to show when these might be developed

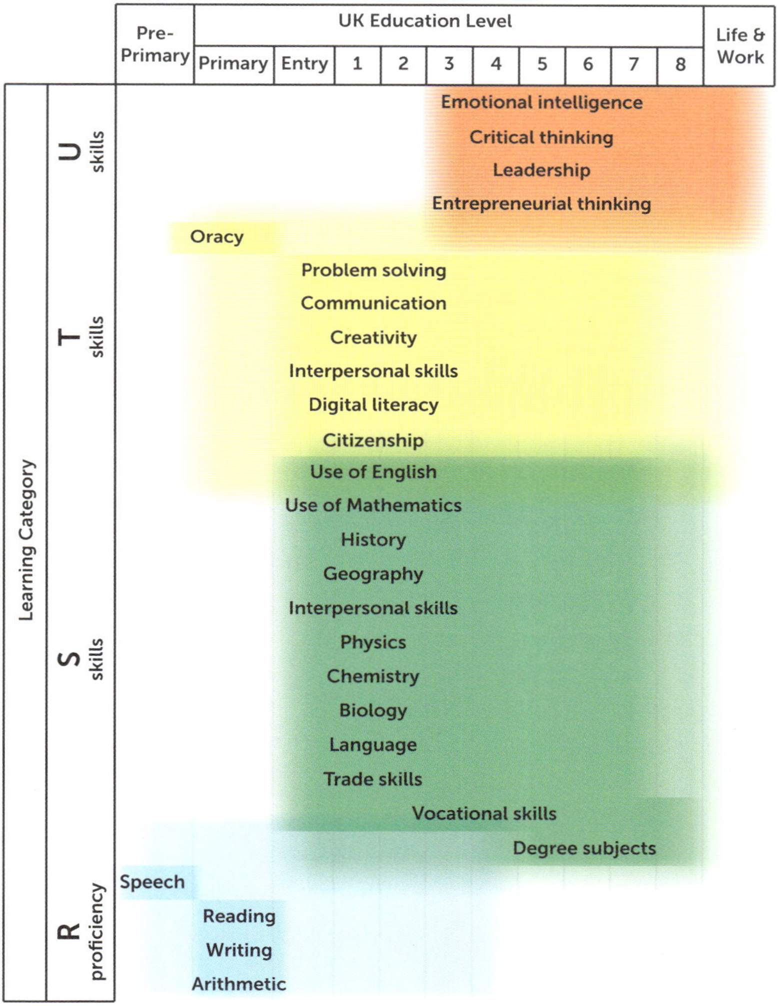

UK education levels 1-3 correspond to secondary school and further education in the UK, while 4-8 are higher education.

Reflection on the 'Map'

The categorisation suggested above not only introduces T and U skills but also provides a vocabulary for discussing the different possible categories of learning.

Explanation of the Map:

- **U skills** include Emotional intelligence, Critical thinking, Leadership and Entrepreneurial thinking. While these are higher-order skills of relevance particularly to higher education (levels 4 and above), they may also be applicable for level 3 students, and certain elements such as entrepreneurial thinking can even be demonstrated as early as primary school. These skills will continue to be developed during life and work.

- **T skills** start at primary school or even earlier for some and include skills such as communication, citizenship, working with others, creativity and digital literacy. These skills are developed particularly during primary school and entry level to level 3 in further education or secondary school. Some skills may continue to be developed throughout life and education.

- **S learning** spans entry-level through to higher education (levels 4-8), with some S learning at primary. It includes use of subjects such as English, history, physics, chemistry, trade and professional skills and degree subjects.

- **R proficiency** includes reading, writing and arithmetic and is intended to be achieved during primary education. However, some students currently progress to levels 1 and above requiring further practice and study in these areas.

As has been recognised, the different suggested T and U skills are not distinct clearly separate entities but more like a spectrum in that different areas can merge into each other and there are no distinct boundaries separating them. Equally, when different skills or categories of learning are addressed may depend on context.

Using this perspective as a way of viewing learning could be beneficial. It could, for instance, both indicate what might be missing and show where abilities other than those traditionally taught would fit into the system.

It is suggested that the learning components needed for employability, enterprise and/or entrepreneurship are essentially T skills, many of which have a much wider application than just in 'business' and would therefore be helpful if included at any level of education provision. However, there are no commonly used and widely accepted definitive lists, either of economic or of wider life-related skills, and neither are the suggested skills all clearly distinct from each other. Nevertheless, they are important and the various lists referenced here provide a starting point.

It might also be argued that there are other categories in addition to R, S, T and U. One candidate might be vocational excellence (therefore V excellence) which can come from experience in applying relevant S learning assisted by T skills in a real vocational setting. But it might also be relevant to acknowledge that experience is only beneficial if it leads to learning and improvement and therefore a breadth of experience can be beneficial: in other words, as is sometimes noted, there is a difference between ten years' experience and one year's experience repeated ten times.

Of course, adopting the R-S-T-U categorisation would not solve all education's issues. It is not a magic cure: the application of which will somehow correct all problems. It is, however, suggested that it would be a helpful first step and the foundation on which further progress could hopefully be made.

Vocabulary, Methods and Assessment

As the earlier chapters show, T (and U) skills are important skills, not only for economic application, but for life generally - and are relevant considerations at all levels of education. However, they have received little formal recognition and, for this, there are probably three main reasons.

One is that there has not been a widely accepted vocabulary to label and identify them - if something does not have a clear name it is hard to recognise and talk about it. A second reason is that people have not been aware of clear methods for developing such skills and have not seen examples they could follow. Then the third reason is that the acquisition of T skills has not been measured, assessed or recorded - and, if people don't have some way of certifying the skills they have, they do not feel they are valued and cannot show proof of them to others.

In Part II of this book, the PBL method for developing T skills is described and illustrated with case studies - and these cases also include examples of the assessment of T skills and a way of recording them. The 'map' above suggests a vocabulary for discussing this range of important skills - but some of the main ones are highlighted and defined or described in section 5.1 and 5.2 and this book endeavours to maintain this use.

5.1 - A vocabulary for different aspects of learning

The three Es

Employability:
The ability to undertake, and suitably maintain, employment on a particular task and in a particular situation.

Enterprise:
A sense of initiative and the ability to have helpful ideas and to turn them into relevant action - in any part of life.

Entrepreneurship:
Unless quoting other uses, this book tries to avoid using the term 'entrepreneurship' because it can be understood in different and even contradictory ways, and therefore often does not communicate a clear consistent message.

Skills and Competencies

The terms skill and competency are often used loosely and even interchangeably - and this should be borne in mind when these words are encountered. However, except when quoting from other sources, the book endeavours to follow this distinction:

Skill:
A skill is the learnt and applied ability to carry out a particular activity. Thus, to be competent at making business decisions requires skills such as budgeting, market research and analysis. Further those skills are transferable and can also be used for other tasks.

Competency:
Being competent at something requires the mix of skill, ability, knowledge and/or attitude needed to be able to do it satisfactorily. Being competent at one task does not however transfer to another.

Categories of learning

R proficiency:
Those basic proficiencies (such as the three Rs of reading, writing and arithmetic) which are a necessary foundation for further learning.

S learning:
The learning typical of much school study which is primarily concerned with the acquisition of knowledge about facts and theories in particular subjects which are often studied in separate 'silos'.

T skills:
The skills needed to live and work well which are not knowledge based or related to a particular activity.

U skills:
Those higher-level skills needed for effective working beyond just being a team member.

5.2 - Some transversal and uber skill sets

Transversal (T) skills

Those skills needed to live and work well but which are not essentially knowledge-based or specifically related to a particular job or task. They include the following skill sets:

Citizenship skills:
Contributing to the community, whether at a small or local (e.g. college or workplace) or wider (e.g. locality/ wide community) level.

Skills for coping with uncertainty:
Understanding risk and complexity and being mentally prepared to face the unexpected.

Skills for working with others:
Being able to communicate both through speaking and writing and to listen to others, to interact with others with empathy, and to work well in a team and participate effectively in group activity.

Problem-solving and decision-making skills:
Being competent in analysing real world situations and problems, generating relevant solutions, and selecting, through evaluation and/or experimentation, the best option and then, where necessary, 'selling' that solution to others.

Creativity skills:
Exploring issues and concepts, using different perspectives, applying lateral thinking, generating new ideas and applying them.

Self-management skills:
The capability to organise and motivate oneself, especially when faced with challenges. This involves self-awareness, self-discipline, an understanding of how to approach risk and uncertainty, resilience, time management and the ability to learn.

Work professionalism skills:
Identifying and exhibiting appropriate behaviour and attitudes for the workplace. This includes punctuality, dressing appropriately, following set policy and procedures, meeting deadlines and balancing work and non-work demands.

Digital literacy skills:
The skills needed to live, work and learn safely in the world today. It involves being able to use digital devices and navigate communication applications and networks and manage information.

Uber (U) skills

Those higher-level transversal skills needed for effective working beyond just being a member of a team.

Emotional intelligence skills:
Being able to understand, manage and use emotions to thrive personally, professionally and socially.

Critical thinking skills:
Having the ability to question apparent theories, beliefs and explanations with an open mind and to explore different arguments and actively and objectively analyse, evaluate and apply information gathered.

Leadership skills:
The skills needed to inspire, motivate, organise and coordinate and thus maximise the contributions of others working together to achieve a common goal more effectively than they would if left to their own devices.

Entrepreneurial thinking skills:
Being able to have and develop helpful ideas and to identify and use opportunities beyond the obvious or routine and to turn them into relevant and successful action.

Experiential learning:
The process of learning through experience. It generally involves more than just acquiring the knowledge necessary to perform a particular activity but also the other skills and abilities necessary to apply the relevant knowledge effectively.

Project Based Learning:
A particular form of experiential learning in which students apply themselves to projects designed to develop the skills they need and for which they are guided/coached while undertaking the project.

References

1 OECD, Learning Compass 2030: A series of concept notes, (OECD Future of Education and Skills 2030, 2019) (www.oecd.org/education/2030-project/teaching-and-learning/learning/learning-compass-2030/ accessed 6 Oct 2023)

2 S. Glasbeek, The Importance of Transversal Skills and Competencies for Young People, (AEGEE Europe Policy Paper, 2018) https://www.aegee.org/policy-paper-the-importance-of-transversal-skills-and-competences-for-young-people-in-a-modern-europe/ accessed 1 Jan 2023

3 UNESCO, Education Policy Brief (Vol.2), 2014: Skills for holistic human developmenthttps://unesdoc.unesco.org/ark:/48223/pf0000245064/PDF/245064eng.pdf.multi (accessed 9 Oct 2023)

4 The Cambridge Life Competencies Framework - Introductory Guide, (Cambridge University Press, 2020) www.cambridge.org/clcf (accessed 27 Dec 2023)

5 Ibid

PART 2

RSTU SKILLS - ASPECTS OF THE RELEVANT NORTHERN IRELAND EXPERIENCE

CHAPTER 6

RECOGNISING TRANSVERSAL SKILLS IN NORTHERN IRELAND

Chapter Summary

Much of the traditional education provision has been designed around qualifications and the need for students to pass the relevant exams. Therefore, the learning and assessment process focusses on those exams and, beyond that, the system's approach to the development of other skills or deep learning has been very limited.

Nevertheless, in Northern Ireland official policy encourages a wider approach, both in schools and in further education, but the legacy of the conventional system, and the lack of a recognised assessment system for other skills, often means that they are overlooked. While there is a declared 'Learning for Life and Work' aspiration for education also with an acknowledgement of the enterprise and employability dimension, this is often not seen as important and measured and not therefore valued.

However, some educational organisations are trying to address this deficiency. The South Eastern Regional College (SERC), for example, has introduced a new learning and assessment system specifically to encourage the acquisition by its students of transversal T skills. Its example is therefore explained in the other chapters in this part of the book.

Introduction

Part I of this book highlights the need for education providers to recognise a range of life requirements including the development of sets of skills which have sometimes been labelled 'transversal' - and this has been recognised in Northern Ireland.

Experience there highlights impediments to the wider official advancement of T skills but also provides examples of relevant initiatives which are succeeding. This chapter indicates some of the background to this before, in the next chapter, describing the example of one organisation trying to advance the relevant work.

Learning and Assessment: The Traditional Approach

The traditional approach to learning and assessment has been to create a curriculum defined by a qualification and from that qualification determine how the learning and assessment should take place.

The qualification is often subdivided into a range of modules with very little connectivity between them in terms of either learning or assessment.

Individual students are then assessed against each of the modules to get a grade or performance level which is averaged to get an overall performance for the programme. This method of assessment is further reinforced by the quality assurance process which looks for the individual student grades. Performance using assessment tools such as public examinations, time-controlled assessments, essays, online examinations using multiple choice questions are driven by the philosophy that there should be a single right answer to a question, assignment or challenge because it is easier to measure.

The result is that traditional assessment:

- Reduces innovation and creativity.
- Focuses upon individual student performance.
- Does not encourage peer learning.
- Does not develop the student's technical skills.
- Does not develop the student's T (and U) skills.
- Does not promote digital pedagogy.
- Treats entrepreneurial activity as an add-on and not core curriculum.
- Does not recognize that students operate in a digital world.

Current Policy

In Schools

In the past it would have been reasonable to say that the primary school sector focussed on the acquisition by pupils of basic skills such as proficiency in the three Rs and the Post-Primary sector on teaching a set of knowledge-based subjects (S learning). However, in Northern Ireland, since 2007, education policy has set out the curriculum for Primary and Post-Primary education, including a cross-curricular approach for the explicit development of 'Thinking Skills and Personal Capabilities'[1].

This recognition in the official curriculum guidance allows educators opportunities to create space in curriculum delivery for the inclusion of practical and vocational opportunities for young people to nurture skills practice. The curriculum refers to the development of 'Whole Curriculum Skills and Capabilities' and, for instance, at Key Stage 3 (children aged 11 to 14), there is a 'Learning for Life and Work' aspiration with an enterprise and employability dimension and a series of key elements such as citizenship, media awareness and economic awareness as well as 'T' skills such as managing information, working with others, problem solving, decision making, self-management and being creative.

While that is the theory, the entrenched legacy of earlier practice and the primacy of R proficiency and then S learning together with established and widely recognised methods for their assessment means that often only lip-service is paid to the more widely applicable transferable skill elements. Therefore, although T skills should be in the school curriculum, they, and with them enterprise and employability education, remain as fringe considerations where progress is thought to be difficult to document and measure and, without assessment, is easy to ignore.

In Further Education

In the Further Education sector also the need for enterprise and employability, and for the associated 'T' skills, has been recognised. For instance:

- It is understood that, in 2016 an internal report by the Department for the Economy Curriculum Development Reform Team drew on skills frameworks from UNESCO and the cross-curricular skills, thinking skills and personal capabilities within the Northern Ireland Curriculum.

- Also in 2016 the then Department for Employment and Learning published its Northern Ireland Strategy for Further Education: *Further Education Means Success,* which spoke of the need to develop 'employability skills' and 'enterprising learners who are innovative and creative and able to adapt to change'[2].

- This fitted well with the 2017 publication of Economy 2030: A Consultation on an Industrial Strategy for Northern Ireland with its vision to create a globally competitive economy[3]. The proposed framework comprised five pillars including accelerating innovation and research, and enhancing skills, education and employability and the articulated priority needs for these included many things for which 'T' skills would be needed.

However, as in the school sector, the lack of measurement and qualifications for the skills and competencies specified has made it harder for them to be valued and to gain recognition and hindered their adoption. This omission was, for instance, noted in 2019 by the Northern Ireland Skills Barometer which highlighted a lack of non-technical, 'soft' or 'transversal' skills such as communication, teamwork and problem solving amongst graduates[4].

In Higher Education

Unlike schools and further education colleges, universities are independent bodies which are not directed by, and/or answerable to, government departments. Therefore, they are not obliged in the same way to follow official policies. The most recent formal HE policy in Northern Ireland, *Graduating to Success*, dates from 2012 and, although it indicates that 'all students should have the opportunity to develop a distinctive portfolio of skills and attributes that will enhance their employability'[5] it does not say more about the skills and attributes likely to be required for this.

Nevertheless, in practice, relevant skills and attributes are developed in HE, not driven by government dictation, but informed by suggested policies and frameworks such as those from:

QAA
The Quality Assurance Agency for Higher Education ('The UK's expert quality body for tertiary education').

AACSB
Association to Advance Collegiate Schools of Business.

PMRE
Principles for Responsible Management Education.

Implementation Examples

In this situation and in response to wider advocacy and to requirements such as those described above, attempts have been made in Northern Ireland to advance the acquisition of 'T' skills - and these are two examples:

Young Enterprise

Young Enterprise has been operating in Northern Ireland for over 30 years. Initially established to help school pupils to learn about business, one of its main vehicles has been its Company Programme in which teams of young people are given the opportunity to set up and run their own student company with guidance from business volunteers.

Over the course of the programme, participants are introduced to the realities of the world of work and gain practical business experience while developing an enterprising mindset and building employability skills. Consequently, without using that vocabulary, YE has for some time been assisting students to develop the T skills now recognised as necessary for employability and enterprise. Further reflections on this are therefore given in chapter 10.

South Eastern Regional College

South Eastern Regional College (SERC) is one of Northern Ireland's six further and higher education colleges and was created in 2007 by the merger of three earlier institutes.

Between them, the colleges are the largest provider of professional and technical qualifications in Northern Ireland. SERC offers a range of full and part-time courses as well as evening part-time leisure courses and has over 30,000 students. As a Further Education (FE) college, SERC is a primary delivery arm for the government policy of ensuring that the Northern Ireland workforce has the skills necessary to build and maintain a successful economy.

However, for some time SERC has been conscious that the traditional methods of education at the 'further' level have not met well the requirements of its students, of existing employers or of those advocating more business creation and growth. Therefore, in 2017, it developed a new learning and assessment model called Project Based Learning (PBL) using a hybrid of the Basque country VET model[6] for challenge-based learning and the Conceive Design Implement and Operate Model developed by the CDIO organisation[7].

The traditional learning assessment model, which had been in use for decades, was not addressing the needs of the College's student population. The focus for many students had been on knowledge and trade skills and not things like innovation and creativity and so did not address the societal context in which the students need to operate. The key elements of the traditional learning and assessment models needed to change to enable innovation and creativity to flourish.

Therefore, the College needed to develop a model which would operate in the context in which it found itself. One of the key measures of performance of further education colleges is the number of qualifications they deliver but, unfortunately, the learning and assessment model built into the curriculum had not progressed sufficiently and did not encourage innovation and creativity in the pedagogy to be utilised. SERC's response was twofold; it has introduced Project Based Learning (PBL) as a way of developing students' T skills and it has developed ways of assessing and recording the performance levels. This approach is described in more detail in the next chapters.

References

1 CCEA, Curriculum Skills and Capabilities, (Belfast: Council for the Curriculum, Examination and Assessment), https://ccea.org.uk/about/what-we-do/curriculum/curriculum-skills-and-capabilities accessed 1 July 2024

2 Further Education Means Success: The Northern Ireland Strategy for Further Education, (Belfast: Department for Education and Learning, January 2016) p.44

3 Economy 2030: A Consultation on an Industrial Strategy for Northern Ireland (Belfast, Department for the Economy, 2017)

4 Ulster University Economic Policy Centre, Northern Ireland Skills Barometer, July 2019

5 Graduating to Success (Belfast: Department for Employment and Learning, 2012)

6 Learning and high performance - Tknika, https://tknika.eus/en/areas-2/learning-and-high-performance/, accessed 9 July 2024.

7 What is a CDIO-based education? | Worldwide CDIO Initiative, http://www.cdio.org/cdio-vision, accessed 9 July 2024

CHAPTER 7

EXPERIENTIAL LEARNING AND DEVELOPING T SKILLS: AN EXAMPLE

Chapter Summary

Aware of the need for its students to acquire relevant T skills, SERC introduced Project Based Learning (PBL). This uses real-life projects to which students are assigned to work in teams with lecturers taking the role of 'guide-on-the-side' rather than 'sage-on the-stage'. It has helped students to develop T skills while also developing appropriate technical and vocational skills within the PBL paradigm.

Significant staff development over time has been crucial to the successful implementation of this PBL model for developing T and vocational skills - and that is unlikely to succeed without it. A framework for the rollout of such a model must also accommodate variations in the attitudes to training in different sectors of work and employment - lessons learned in one sector may apply in others and flexibility is required.

For SERC the results have justified the effort involved. Not only has vocational skills development been enhanced but T skills have been developed in an integrated methodology and both have been assessed. It has also been observed that students are more motivated, better prepared for work and their retention rates have also improved. Staff are also highly motivated once they understand how to plan and implement the PBL model.

Introduction

As previously indicated, South Eastern Regional College (SERC) is one of the six further and higher education colleges which, between them, are the largest provider of professional and technical qualifications in Northern Ireland.

However, for some time SERC has been conscious that the traditional methods of education at the 'further' level have not met well the requirements of its students, of existing employers or of those wanting to enhance business creation and growth. This chapter describes its response.

The Background to a New Learning Model

It became clear to SERC that modern jobs need new skill sets which were not required in the past. Jobs are evolving and long-term job opportunities are no longer as prevalent as they were.

To keep pace with this transformation in the economic and social landscape, transversal skills need to become part of the curriculum in order to ensure that students have not just the knowledge, but also the skills, attitudes and behaviours needed to thrive in life and work today.

Transversal Skills

SERC was aware of a growing body of research which had shown a gap between the skills learnt at school and those needed for life and work in the 21st century. For example, the Northern Ireland Skills Barometer[1] highlighted a lack of non-technical, 'soft' or 'transversal' skills, such as communication, teamwork and problem-solving, amongst graduates - and businesses need graduates with these skills to help drive growth and innovation. Also UNESCO (The United Nations Educational Scientific and Cultural Organisation) has identified the critical role of Transversal Skills for effective participation in life and work in a hyper-connected knowledge society and suggested five examples of such skills.

- Critical and innovative thinking
- Inter-personal skills e.g., presentation and communication, organisational skills, and teamwork
- Intra-personal skills e.g., self-discipline, enthusiasm, perseverance, and self-motivation
- Global citizenship e.g., tolerance, openness, respect for diversity and intercultural understanding
- Media and information literacy such as the ability to locate and access information, as well as analyse and evaluate media content.[2]

Therefore, guided by a 2016 internal report on transversal skills from the Northern Ireland Department for the Economy Curriculum Development Reform team (which drew both on the work of UNESCO and the Northern Ireland curriculum guidance), SERC produced its own plans for the T skills it wished to introduce (illustrated in Figure 7.1).

Figure 7.1 - SERC's Transversal Skills Diagram

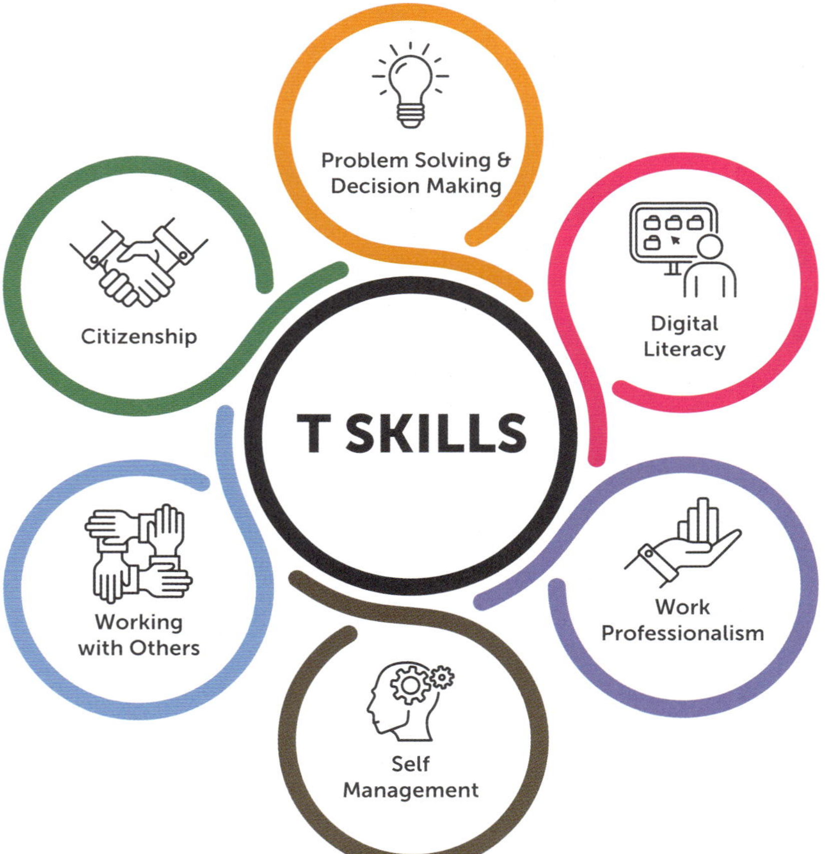

Figure 7.1 not only shows the six sets of T skills recognised by SERC but also indicates their relationship to each other. There are no hard boundaries to the sets mentioned and, for example, work professionalism can be aided by digital literacy skills as well as by self-management - and it can therefore usefully be developed alongside them.

The Learning Requirement

SERC perceived that, although T skills are critical to success in a wide variety of situations, interactions and work settings; typically they are not specifically related to a given job, academic discipline or area of knowledge. These skills are increasingly in high demand for individuals to adapt successfully to change, to lead meaningful and productive lives and to develop a sense of "boundary less mobility".

T skills should be a core part of the further education curriculum which, SERC believed, should also include the vocational skills traditionally taught in Further Education, literacy and numeracy for those students lacking an adequate ability in that area, and enterprise and 'entrepreneurship' skills for students who might wish to start their own ventures.

Project Based Learning

Consequently, the College developed a model which would be appropriate for the context in which it found itself by helping its students to acquire T skills fully integrated with the traditional work-related skills. SERC understood that T skills are best acquired through experiential learning: through coached practice and not from classroom-based knowledge assimilation. Therefore, it introduced a new learning method based on Project Based Learning (PBL).

In this the students work in teams to undertake practical real-world projects under the guidance of appropriately prepared staff. Using a PBL pedagogy SERC was then able to deliver a more complete learning environment as illustrated in Figure 7.2.

Figure 7.2 - Towards a Complete Education

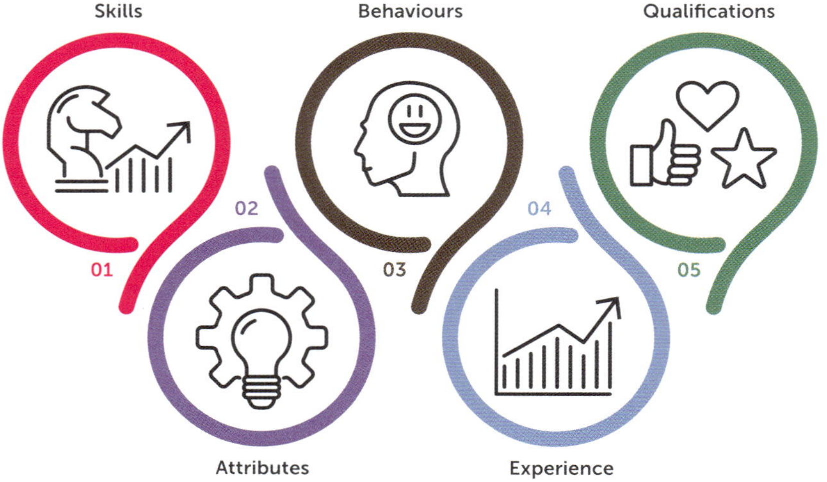

PBL in Action

SERC's PBL learning model has 12 stages - illustrated in Figure 7.3 below. In this, students are first assessed and then assigned to work in groups on predesigned industry or society related projects relevant to their area of study and in which both vocational and T skills are developed and assessed.

Figure 7.3 - SERC's Model for Project-Based Learning PBL Projects

The first stage in following a PBL strategy is to develop appropriate projects that support acquisition of the qualification to be obtained. The pedagogy should ensure that the students are working in groups on projects that are sufficiently open-ended to enable the output from the project to be student centred. This is a significant challenge for many staff who have been conditioned to create projects for students with a single correct outcome.

The basic principles are:

- Projects must have a real-world scenario or be an industry challenge. This contextualisation ensures students can understand the value and impact of their projects.

- Projects should be designed to integrate T skills alongside technical and professional skills. The evidence for T skills should then be naturally occurring from the PBL projects without generating extra burden for both staff and student.

- Projects may be organised as small projects leading to larger projects over the duration of the learning programme. Projects must be open-ended to allow different solutions to be produced by each team.

- The projects may combine teams from different occupational areas.

PBL Teaching Teams

Prior preparation is essential for PBL teaching teams. This should ensure that existing curriculum learning objectives are covered while at the same time changing the learning model. Some of the behaviours of staff need to change dramatically: for example they need to believe that students can do the work and that lecturers (mentors) are there to facilitate. The lecturer may also at times become part of a student team.

A preliminary to the application of the new PBL model is the significant re-training which staff are required to undertake. They need to move away from the individual or silo-based delivery of modules to a team approach: planning PBL activities that cross multiple modules. Smaller teaching teams of three to four staff make this more realisable and effective. As well as facilitating the delivery of learning, the lecturer must act as a moderator and intervene if the student team is not functioning properly.

Students in PBL Teams

An important part of the PBL experience for students is working in teams with their peers. Students should be profiled so that each group has a mixture of students including both those with a strength in organisation skills and those who are creative and entrepreneurial. This will help ensure the success of the team and the interaction between the team members.

Students should be encouraged to take responsibility for their own learning. They should discuss a range of solutions to the project challenge and analyse these options against the constraints of the project. The constraints may include time, resources and other design boundaries. The student team should then present their best solution at an appropriate venue.

SERC has found that, as skills are developed, students start to modify behaviours and attitudes to their peers, tutors and to learning and assessment. Experience gained through work-based learning placements or employment further enhances the students' skills and reinforces positive attitudes and behaviours.

Enterprise Fortnight and Student Exposition (Expo):

A key element at the start of the PBL exercise is Enterprise Fortnight. This happens in the first two weeks of term in September each year and its purpose is to create disruption to the traditional learning model as well as to integrate the student into college life and accelerate peer bonding within their cohort. During this time, having been formed into teams, students complete a first iteration of their task and will demonstrate the work they have completed at the PBL exposition (Expo) where all students exhibit their projects in the public areas on their campus.

At the Expo, students are judged by a panel of 'experts' (internal and external to the College) and given constructive feedback. It is important to note that at this stage it is not just the best project group in the cohort that go to the expo - all students get the opportunity. This gives students and staff the opportunity to see the work produced across the College and is a key element in incrementally improving the quality of the projects developed.

The use of public spaces is extremely important to ensure that all students are given the opportunity to celebrate their achievements. It moves the learning and assessment from the classroom to a much more engaging, dynamic and sensory experience in the public spaces for both staff and students.

College staff may merge first and second year groups during the enterprise fortnight which encourages the transfer of knowledge from second to first year students. Lecturers are encouraged to work across departmental boundaries, for example, engineers may work with catering or performing arts.

This type of cross fertilisation encourages true innovation and can result in spectacularly successful and innovative projects.

The Enterprise Fortnight does create additional logistic demands because of the huge number of students and staff involved. The organisers normally schedule students over two or three days in the four major campuses to ensure that all students have the opportunity to exhibit and participate. The judging of the enterprise Fortnight also requires significant input. Judges are briefed on how to approach the judging process and asked to make their comments as constructive as possible to build student confidence and encourage further development. For some students, this may be the first time they have received positive feedback for work they have completed so confidence building is a critical component of the Expo.

Learning and Assessment Through PBL

The focus for PBL pedagogy in the FE sector should be on the development of skills, which include both vocational learning and T skills. As with all skill development, students need time and repeated practice repeatedly to develop fully a confident skill level.

The range of projects within a learning programme must be mapped for the complete year. A range of assessment strategies should complement the series of projects and include peer, audience and self-assessment. Learning objectives may be covered more than once to enable students to develop their skills more deeply. Assessment should cover both technical and T skills through 'naturally-occurring evidence'.

Assessment (see also Chapter 9) should be continuous with the lecturer providing regular feedback and scaffolding the students to the next level of skills development. In some subject areas, a synoptic skills test can be included to ensure that the students can demonstrate the range of skills developed over time. The skills test also helps provide individual assessment for the student. As with all continuous assessment on group activity, regular constructive feedback is vital to appraise the student of his or her progress and set out their next direction of travel.

The final step for students is the attainment of recognised qualifications which are seen as the 'by-product of learning'. It is important to stress the sequencing of this model as too often in traditional learning and assessment models it seems that the qualification dictates rather than complements the learning and assessment process.

The SERC Example

The following paragraphs highlight some salient aspects of SERC's PBL experience:

Project Themes

Figure 7.4 - Themes for Project-Based Learning at SERC

To enhance the design of the projects used in PBL, SERC has developed a range of project themes (see Figure 7.4) to provide a focus for tutor teams whilst at the same time providing scope for potential project areas. Using these themes to design the projects should make the presentation of project outcomes more coherent and easier to judge and assess. SERC delivers qualifications in over 50 different vocational areas, so a coherent focus was needed for the development of projects by both staff and students. Using the project themes also meant that judging was easier to organise.

Continuous Professional Development of Staff

It is important to focus on the development of pedagogy skills required for the implementation of a PBL approach. Significant time and resources are required to ensure staff are guided through the process and given time to develop the skills to transform traditional learning assessment methodologies to a PBL pedagogy. This move can be difficult and takes a long time for the majority of staff.Staff development is a fundamental element in the implementation of a PBL strategy and Continuous Professional Development (CPD) is a key component in the implementation of PBL in SERC. CPD in SERC involves many strategies including intensive 10-day full-time programmes as well as PBL mentors who work with teams through the year. Without this, CPD will not happen except in an *ad hoc* or sporadic fashion.

CPD enables staff to unlearn some of the deeply ingrained traditional pedagogy they have used over the years and to relearn the new skills required for the PBL pedagogy such as planning and collaboration within the delivery team. A good analogy for this is the competence hierarchy (see Figure 7.5).

If one considers the change in skills required in riding a motorcycle to driving a car then the change is quite dramatic. Both are using a motorised vehicle on public roads with other users. One requires a greater degree of balance and control and the rider is more exposed to the environment and prone to accidents. The other is more cocooned in a bubble, environment factors are not as acute and risk of injury from accidents dramatically reduced.

Both skills begin as:

- unconscious incompetence
- then the progression to the desire to ride/drive - moves to conscious incompetence
- conscious competence is ability to carry out the skill but with a conscious effort
- finally unconscious competence is ability to perform the skill without thinking

Figure 7.5 - Hierarchy of Competence

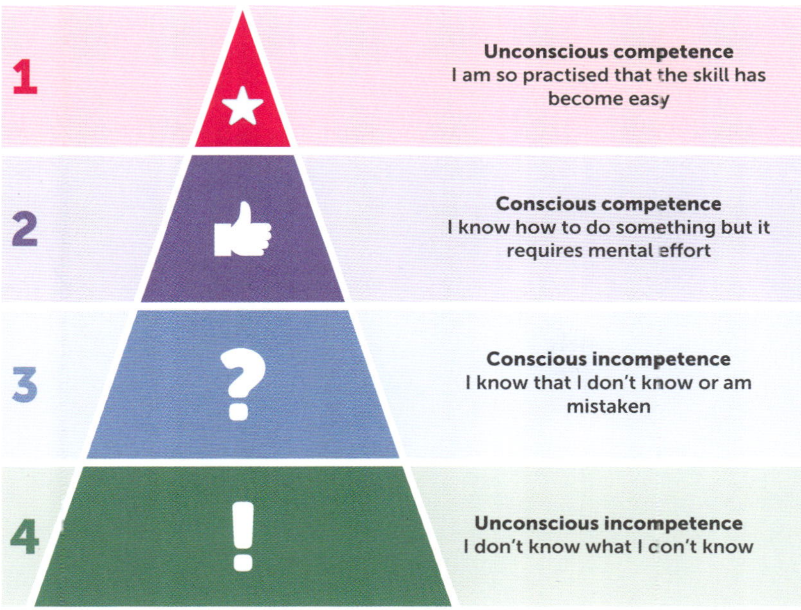

New Lecturer Induction

To move away from the traditional methods of curriculum delivery staff working with PBL need to develop a different range of skills. Therefore, newly appointed staff are specifically trained in the SERC PBL principles and processes and supported in this by initiatives such as:

- **PBL mentors** - carefully selected and trained staff who work with teams to develop an implementation plan and review progress of PBL within specific disciplines.

- **Intensive PBL CPD** - whole sections of staff in specific disciplines who are intensively trained in PBL and who are tasked with developing PBL within their vocational area for immediate implementation - usually taking place in August.

- **Ongoing PBL staff development** - for example, amendments and updates to SERC PBL strategy or specific technologies to aid or improve the PBL implementation process.

Planning and Collaborative Skills

Traditional curriculum design has often resulted in the creation of programmes of learning which are comprised of a series of components. This type of curriculum often creates a silo based delivery of learning and assessment. Students often have difficulty in connecting the learning between the different modules because of the lack of overarching themes or projects.

The traditional approach to the assessment of learning is also a problem because in addition to individual assessment of the modules within a programme we also have individual assessment of the student. This is driven by the mistaken belief that individual assessment of students is difficult to achieve from group projects.

Staff need to develop new skills around the planning of a more integrated approach to the delivery and assessment of PBL projects. This will include developing several projects and mapping those projects to existing curriculum structures such as modules or units. They will also need to plan how the student group projects are to be delivered and structured over the academic year. This requires the whole teaching team to work in collaboration through a series of meetings where project options are discussed to ensure that all the learning objectives of the programme can be achieved.

PBL Skills

Delivery staff need to revisit how the projects are created. For example, projects must provide a stimulating and fun learning experience for the students. The projects should be open-ended so that students have more input into the solution to the project that has been assigned.

It is also important that the projects focus on skills development. An example of this might be a project within a science curriculum that allows the students to develop laboratory and testing skills rather than focus on a purely academic research project that is desk based. Also in engineering fabrication, students might focus on creating products from upcycled materials or products that can then be sold at a student fair. Students then have a focus on developing vocational skills such as welding so that the product meets an acceptable standard for retail.

Other areas of relevant staff skills include:

- Innovative and creative thinking skills including working across different professional and technical areas.
- Pedagogical skills including knowing how different students learn, knowing how to mentor and support student PBL teams and providing continuous assessment and positive feedback.
- Technology enhanced learning skills including supporting learning and assessment and supporting students with technical issues.

Evaluating SERC's Approach

In 2022, to provide independent feedback on the College's efforts, researchers at Stranmillis University College conducted an evaluation of Project Based Learning at SERC. Among the findings of their report were the following:

- 'Student survey results overwhelmingly demonstrated significantly positive benefit attributed directly to the PBL experience across every category of transversal skills as defined by SERC'.
- The results also showed that, as direct result of the PBL experience, 19% of [participating] students intended to start a

business - compared to an average rate of 'early-stage entrepreneurship' of 6.5% in Northern Ireland.

- 'Staff survey results showed significantly increased enjoyment of teaching and improved efficacy of student learning.' 'Staff considered PBL experiences to be very strongly supportive of transversal skill development and affirmed that transversal skills were more valuable for some 'real world' applications than traditional classroom practice.'[3]

Case Study 7.1

PBL: A Woodworking Example

Overview

This example is a project for students on the Level 2 Diploma in Woodworking Skills (OCNNI) course. In the past, teaching and learning have been organised according to the qualification, which is subdivided into modules, learning outcomes and assessment criteria, often with little explicit connectivity between them.

In practice, this meant lecturers setting students stand-alone tasks such as building a doorframe in the workshop, only to then take it down and move on to the next task. Students would perform a task decided by the lecturer in order to learn a specific skill and evidence that learning outcome. Then, they would begin a new task in order to complete the qualification. This approach was somewhat disjointed and offered students little opportunity for autonomy, enterprise, creative thinking or self-initiative. Crucially, it did not adequately support the development of transversal skills or bridge the gap between learning and working environments, resulting in limited motivation among students at times.

In 2022, the curriculum team decided to transition from the teacher-led approach to a more integrated PBL approach, offering students greater agency, decision-making and real-world relevance. The curriculum team developed "real-world" projects for the trainees and apprentices which would allow them to develop and evidence their technical skills while working to deliver a meaningful outcome beyond the classroom.

The 'Garden Room' project described below is an example of a PBL project which has supported carpentry and joinery students, not only to develop technical skill and achieve their formal qualification, but also to develop the transversal skills needed to successfully deploy their learning in different contexts.

The Garden Room Project

An example of one such project was the Garden Room. For this the apprentices and trainees were given this real-world scenario. A client had an open space to the rear of their property which they would like to utilise as a place to sun themselves but also for storage. Working in teams, the students were asked to design and create a structure that would meet both those needs.

The students were given constraints such as timeframe, budget, and types of resources. They followed the steps below to realise the project, which naturally completed various aspects of their qualification. In this case, lecturers had also found clients (colleagues) who were eager to purchase the structures, providing the students with a meaningful and motivating outcome to work towards. The lecturers took the role of "guide-on-the-side" rather than "sage-on-the-stage", allowing students to develop agency, self-efficacy and initiative.

There were also some design constraints such as a budget for materials as well as it being able to be transport the end product in flat pack format. Student groups were asked to address issues such as disassembly as well as choice of design to meet the constraints of the project. Students developed transversal skills such as working together, work professionalism and problem solving and decision making through this group activity.

Project Steps

This project included the following steps

- Students were assigned to teams with diverse skillsets.
- Each student developed a design proposal for the garden room.
- In their teams, students discussed the different proposals, using their project constraints and requirements to help them identify the most appropriate (or the best combination of proposals).
- The students each developed a list of resources and tools needed (with guidance from lecturers).
- Students developed a project plan with help from lecturers.
- Students completed the manufacture of the Garden Room as four sub-projects.

NB Each student needed to do steps 2 and 4 themselves for their qualification. Some students used digital tools, supporting their digital skills. In some cases, the client had a specific request, such as the integration of a PVC door, which students took into consideration. Although the resources and tools had to be pre-ordered as per the logistics of a college, it was very beneficial for students to think through what materials they need as this is something they would have to do in a work context. Lecturers guided decisions towards what was available.

Assessment

A PBL approach requires careful planning at the start of the academic year. Curriculum teams need to work together to agree and plan the projects that students will do and how these map back to the qualification learning outcomes and assessment criteria. (An example of this assessment mapping for the Garden Room project is in Chapter 9.)

Outcomes

An outcome of the project was that the students successfully designed and produced ten garden rooms (see Figure 7.6), seven of which have been sold at the time of writing.

Figure 7.6 - A Completed Garden Room

Lecturers particularly noted increased motivation and initiative on the part of students to carry out their Garden Room Project, compared to the previous cohort of students who had been taught in the traditional, teacher-led style. This motivation was reflected in improved student retention rates. In 2021-22, the apprentices' retention rate was 68%, which rose to 78% in 2022-23 and to 93% in 2023-24 after the introduction of PBL including the Garden Room.

The curriculum team who developed and delivered the PBL approach also noted that:

'The PBL project had a significant impact on students in various ways. The project got students to think critically and solve problems independently and collectively in their groups, which in turn meant that they learnt the importance of communication. They had more responsibility than the old National Vocational Qualification (NVQ) qualification offered them and it made learning more interesting for each of them. The project gave them all ownership and as a result they were motivated to ensure they completed the tasks to the highest standards that their skill sets would allowed. The PBL model has contributed to improvement in student retention as well as developing the skills they need in the real world.

From overseeing the transition from the previous awarding body (which used typical assessment practices) to handing over ownership to students (through setting scenarios and providing support), I can say that the overall end product has been a team that is enthused and motivated to complete their works to the highest quality with all students gaining an insight into what is required in a real world setting. Students have also had the opportunity to develop deeper and higher level of thinking and top embrace the entrepreneurial skills that they have.

The Garden Room project has allowed students to come up with ideas and concepts and bring these to fruition thanks to a suitably challenging project that also meets the awarding body requirements resulting in a tangible outcome for all concerned.

The integration of Project Based Learning into their new OCN NI Level 2 Diploma in Woodworking Skills qualification ignited the students' motivation as they enthusiastically designed, drew and constructed a full-size Garden Room. This hands-on approach not only honed their skills but also empowered them to apply their knowledge in a tangible and fulfilling project.'

References

1 Northern Ireland Skills Barometer (2021 Update), pp38, July 2014, https://www.economy-ni.gov.uk/sites/default/files/publications/economy/ Skills-Barometer-2021-Summary-Report.pdf, (accessed 10 July 2024)

2 UNESCO, Integrating transversal competencies in education policy and practice, (UNESCO: Bangkok, 2014)

3 M. Ievers, B. Cummins and M. Ballentine, Evaluation Report of Project-Based Learning (PBL) at South Eastern Regional College (SERC) Northern Ireland, (Belfast: Stranmillis University College, March 2022)

CHAPTER 8

DEVELOPING UBER SKILLS AND ENTERPRISE

Chapter summary

Chapter 5 introduced a 'map' suggesting a way of categorising the different educational outputs that people might usefully acquire as a preparation for life. As well as the more traditional R proficiencies and S learning, the map includes not only T but also U skills.

This chapter looks at the Uber, or U skills, which, like T skills, are not deliberately fostered by the current education system. It summarises the efforts in Northern Ireland by SERC to recognise and develop these skills including critical thinking, emotional intelligence, leadership and entrepreneurial thinking.

In recognition that entrepreneurial thinking can often lead to business ideas, it also shows how such initiatives can be encouraged to explore that route.

Introduction

Chapter 5 introduced a 'map' suggesting a way of categorising the different skills that people might usefully acquire as a preparation for life. As well as the more traditional R proficiencies and S learning, the map includes not only T but also U skills.

As the previous chapter indicates, T skills are critical to success in a wide variety of situations and are not typically considered to be related to a given occupation or area of knowledge. While it may have been customary to acquire some of these skills through experience rather than formal education, it is suggested that the education system should recognise them and endeavour to ensure that the need for them is addressed.

It is likely, however, as the earlier chapters of this book indicate, that there are gaps in the current education system - and that the more salient gaps will be in the provision of Transversal and Uber Skills - T skills and U skills. Recognising that students undertaking Further or Higher Education courses often experience a different learning experience, and are more prone to be working independently and seeking graduate opportunities, SERC also encourages the development of higher level skills called Uber or U skills.

U Skills

The label U skills recognises those higher order skills which evolve from the T skills underpinning all learning at SERC. There are four such key skill sets which are particularly encouraged within SERC that progress from the T skill development.

- Critical Thinking
- Emotional Intelligence
- Leadership
- Entrepreneurial thinking.

Critical Thinking

Critical thinking skills enable us reflectively to question theories, beliefs and explanations with an open mind. Graduates critically explore different arguments to actively apply, analyse, and evaluate information gathered objectively. In particular, critical thinking includes:

- Interpreting evidence, data and arguments and evaluating sources.
- Actively listening to and identifying the significance of a question or task.
- Developing well-reasoned arguments using, drawing on and analysing evidence researched to justify conclusions or ideas, referencing sources appropriately and protecting the data and identity of others.

- Synthesising own thoughts and the thoughts of different authors, research, or theorists.
- Discriminating between useful and less useful details or data to solve PBL challenges (including online research).
- Using logical thought to determine the best solution to a PBL challenge.
- Acknowledging changing circumstances or new information and adapting approach accordingly.
- Identifying and analysing risk/rewards in terms of personal and professional development.
- Extrapolating from information from others, acknowledging different perspectives.

Emotional Intelligence

Emotional Intelligence skills enable us to understand, manage and use our emotions to thrive personally, professionally, and socially. As well as self-motivation, controlling impulse and managing stress, emotional intelligence includes recognising and adapting to the needs, emotions, and perspectives of others for positive outcomes.

This involves, for example:

- Recognising and regulating own emotions, using strategies and tools as required, to support own wellbeing and goals as well as those of others.
- Recognising the needs and emotions of others, using strategies and tools as required, and adapting own approach when appropriate for positive outcomes.
- Using non-verbal communication such as body language appropriately and constructively.

- Considering the perspectives of others and reflecting before acting in moments of heightened emotion, selecting the most constructive action.
- Controlling impulse and delaying gratification in pursuit of long-term goals.
- Managing conflict with sensitivity, empathy and understanding.
- Sharing best practice when appropriate, taking a supportive and constructive approach.

Leadership

Leadership skills enable us to inspire, motivate and maximise the efforts of others to achieve positive, common goals. Leadership skills, such as the following, provide a basis for us to work effectively with others to drive change and deliver results in a timely manner, while behaving professionally and ethically:

- Creativity and the ability to inspire change and influence others.
- Being a coach and mentor to support others, building diverse and inclusive teams and maximising the efforts of others.
- Demonstrating integrity and treating others with fairness and respect.
- Seeking opinion and inviting feedback, adopting and modelling a positive, solutions-focused attitude.
- Being able to turn information and data into action.
- Being able to deliver outcomes in changing circumstances, including by adopting a flexible approach to how outcomes are delivered, allowing action plans to be amended and updated.
- Facilitating change by creating conditions that support innovation and by removing common barriers faced by teams.

- The ability to communicate complex information in a clear and concise manner.
- Managing actions of self and others to deliver results.
- Provide vision and direction to others.

Entrepreneurial Thinking

Entrepreneurial thinking enables us to identify and capitalise on opportunities and to manage risk effectively. As well as demonstrating a strong work ethic and the drive to succeed, entrepreneurs are innovative, creative and seek to solve problems. This can involve:

- Using innovation to solve challenges.
- Following through on the work required to turn ideas and projects into services or sellable products.
- Managing time to meet multiple demands, prioritising effectively.
- Assessing the social and environmental consequences of ideas and goals to create sustainable solutions and act responsibly.
- Showing focus and determination when faced with challenges or setbacks.
- Adopting a flexible approach to decision-making and challenges.
- Being persuasive to get backing from investors or industry.
- Identifying and managing risk and taking measured risks for potential return.
- Making decisions when the outcome of a decision is uncertain.
- Growing professional networks.
- Learning from experience and accepting and acting on feedback.

Building Business Enterprise

Entrepreneurial thinking does not automatically lead to the formation of new businesses, but it can lead to enterprising students seeing an opportunity and/or developing a desire to start or grow a business venture - through the stages portrayed in Figure 8.1. SERC therefore recognises and encourages this transition and supports it.

Figure 8.1 - From Being Enterprising to Becoming Entrepreneurs

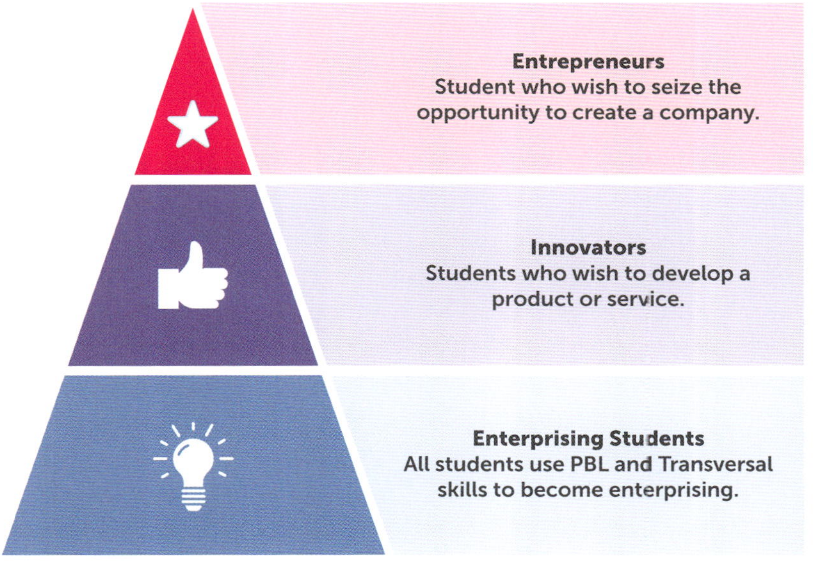

Entrepreneurs Club and Student Companies

The Expo can identify potential projects that could progress to become a student company. Therefore, where appropriate, through the College's Entrepreneur Club, students can set up a student company with the aim of further developing their ideas into real commercial enterprises. The club supports students with innovative or business ideas, provides them with mentoring, workshops and networking opportunities. As a result, it is a significant strength that the College has supported the development of 84 student companies to date, across a range of different vocational areas.

Innovation Advisors

The College tried a variety of methods for using existing teaching staff to help support entrepreneurial development. This had limited success because of the competing demands upon their time with a significant teaching load.

An alternative approach was the appointment of dedicated Innovation Advisors managed by a highly motivated member of the teaching staff with a real flair for developing student businesses. The Innovation Advisors operate independently of the teaching staff, and have a total focus on driving innovation, creativity, enterprise and entrepreneurship with the student entrepreneurs. This alternative approach has been extremely effective across all of the 50 disciplines within the curriculum portfolio at SERC.

Entrepreneur in Residence

To help develop and support student entrepreneurs the College appointed an external expert and practising entrepreneur as the 'Entrepreneur in Residence'. This role enabled students to link into the rich network of contacts for help with specific problems or for provide guidance and business development opportunities. The Entrepreneur in Residence meets with the students on a regular basis through the Entrepreneur Club. The focus is always on practical aspects and developing their company and unlike many other entrepreneurial support systems does not focus on developing business plans.

Themed Fairs for Students

The College introduced a number of innovative initiatives to create opportunities for students to sell their products or services to the public. Student fairs were held at defined points in the year such as Halloween, Christmas, St Valentine's Day, spring and summer. These fairs were held in public areas of the College and provided opportunity to sell products. The interaction with the public at these regular points in the year enable the students to develop segmentation of their products to target the event in time. It also enabled the students to develop excellent communication and negotiation skills as they bartered for package deals - ideal opportunities for evidence of student T skills development.

Supporting U Skill Development

An Open/Growth Mindset

To develop the higher order U skills, it is important that students have an open mindset. A mindset is a deep-rooted perspective on the world and oneself that informs a person's actions and behaviour.

Mindsets are developed over time, through interactions with people and the world. Often, this process is unconscious, however mindsets can be consciously developed through self-reflection and practising certain thoughts and behaviour. Mindsets have a significant role in how we govern ourselves and our emotions, how we approach challenges and obstacles, and how we engage with other people and wider society.

A fixed or closed mindset is typically rooted in negative thinking patterns, where one may perceive challenges as insurmountable and success as something unattainable. An open or growth mindset, however, perceives challenges as opportunities for development, and sees success as an attainable goal, achievable through effort. A person with a fixed mindset believes 'I can't' whereas a person with a growth mindset believes 'I can, and I will" (see also Figure 8.2).

Mindsets can be consciously or unconsciously shaped through development of new skills, and access to opportunities and new experiences. T and U skills help shape existing mindsets into a growth mindset, one which is open to challenges, which meets obstacles head on, and is continuously learning and developing.

Figure 8.2 - The Contrast Between Fixed and Growth Mindsets

Fixed	Growth
I can't	I can and I will
There's no point	I will learn from this
I'm not good enough	My efforts count
I won't be successful	I will be successful
I only see challenge and no opportunity	I see opportunity in challenge
I am scared of failure	I don't fear failure
I will no be able to learn	I want to learn more
I struggle to work with others	I listen to others and learn from them

Practising T and U skills develops patterns of behaviour, which in turn, promote the development of further positive mindsets. Positive behaviours and mindsets help us to improve

The U Skills Framework

Developing attitudes, behaviours and skills that promote success in an individual's life is the key goal of the U Skills Framework. The U Skills Framework expands on the learner's previous T

Skills experiences and encourages the individual to undertake more complex activities. Such activities within the FE and HE context are often new to the learner and seen as outside their comfort zone, while also requiring significant time commitments and/or additional work outside of set class time, such as ensuring academic rigour and research activities.

FE and HE students are expected to become progressively more independent, and responsible for their own learning. The further development of T skills and U skills becomes increasingly pertinent in ensuring that students have the underpinning skillsets within which to operate at a higher level of academia, and therefore be more ready to enter industry. Whilst the U skills focus on the experience of Higher Education students (typically identified as Level 4 and above), U skills may also be applicable for Level 3 students, whose curriculum creates opportunities for development of the U skills (e.g., Adult Education courses with a focus on independent learning and self-direction).

Supporting and Tracking

Understanding and tracking T and U skills development is essential to ensure that every student achieves their potential in life and work.

Well-designed vocational programmes fully integrate and complement the development of mindsets, U skills and T skills, capturing naturally occurring evidence that supports a student's performance level. In addition to core curriculum delivery, activities such as work placements, student companies and extra-curricular pursuits provide ideal opportunities for the development and evidencing of T and U skills.

A growing body of research shows that supporting students in reflecting on and understanding development routes is key to ensuring that they fulfil their potential[1]. In recognition of this, SERC has developed its T and U skills frameworks to create opportunities for self-assessment and reflection.

The U skills are designed to be viewed holistically, with students and teachers aiming to develop and grow their U skills in their learning, life and work.

Environmental and Social Considerations

Two of the key themes used in the development of PBL projects are the environment and wellbeing. Feedback from students identified these as important issues for the student body, which would then get student buy-in more readily. They also enable students to develop open-ended projects with defined constraints and support them to achieve immediate positive outcomes in a very short space of time.Entrepreneurial activities are often seen by a large number of students as capitalistic in nature. This can be off-putting for a large number of them. SERC encourages student entrepreneurs to consider social enterprises as a route which would avoid any clash with their beliefs or ethos.

Some students also use 'wellbeing' as a focus for their projects. This ties in with the approach adopted within the College for the general student body where students are encouraged to have a healthy lifestyle.

Case Study 8.1

PBL: A Health And Social Care Example

Overview
In recognition that uber (U) skills are often needed when working in the healthcare sector, students of Level 4 HNC Healthcare Practice and Social Community Care were supported in mapping their U skills development to their "portfolio of evidence". As part of their course, students undertake work placement and collate evidence of their vocational skills development. Students were supported to identify where they had developed U skills and to reflect on this development.

NB in this context the following are recognised as U skills:

- emotional intelligence
- critical thinking
- leadership
- entrepreneurial thinking

The Health and Social Care Example

The Level 4 Healthcare Practice and Social Community Care programme includes both learning in college and 235 hours of paid employment or work placement. When introducing U skills to this programme, lecturers found that the skills were generally well covered by the specified qualification learning outcomes and by the professional standards and ethics frameworks, to which students must adhere during work placement. However, it was decided that the missing element was the students' ability to *recognise* and *articulate* their development of these skills, which is needed for career progression and further development of the skills.

As part of their programme, students must collate evidence of their development of vocational skills during work placement in digital portfolios. This may include employer testimonies as well as their own reflection and evidence. The concept of uber skills was introduced to students on completion of their portfolios as staff felt it might be too much for students to present them alongside learning outcomes (LOs) and professional standards at the course outset. Also, as stated above, staff found that U skills were already covered by the LOs and standards and so there was less need to explicitly explain them in advance of learning and practice.

References

1 For example N. Duval-Couetil, (2013); Assessing the Impact of Entrepreneurship Education Programmes: Challenges and Approaches', Journal of Small Business Management, Vol.51, Issue 3, pp.394-409 and T. Spielhofer & S. Lynch, (2008). Assessing enterprise capability: Guidance for schools. (Slough: National Foundation for Educational Research)

CHAPTER 9

ASSESSING T AND U SKILLS

Chapter Summary

This chapter reports some of the challenges faced by SERC in providing assessments of the students' acquisition of T and U skills. Developing these skills is more like learning sports than traditional classroom subjects and assessments neec to evaluate practical ability rather than retained knowledge.

Therefore examinations are not appropriate and SERC instead developed a tutor and student observation and recording process, for which examples are given.

The Need for Appropriate Assessments

As Chapter 5 indicates, the lack of a clear and established assessment system appears to be one of the obstacles to a wider acceptance of transversal and uber skills in the education system.

When it comes to assessing learning, it has been suggested that educators need to know that any assessment that they are delivering is trustworthy, curriculum planners need to know how they are to assess the learning outcomes that the course is designed to deliver, and students (and their future employers) need to trust that the assessments provided are useful and valuable to them.[1]

An important part of the T and U skills integration in SERC is therefore the methodology employed to assess the performance level of students. The traditional method of educational assessment has been by written examination but that is applicable for knowledge-based subjects (S learning) not for T and U skills. T and U skills are much more like sports where prowess can really only be assessed on the pitch. Therefore, SERC has adopted a combination of tutor observations and student self-assessment as the practical and appropriate method.

This assessment is continuous throughout the programme with tutors carrying out very regular assessment of the students' skills performance level and recording supporting evidence, while students record their own evidence summary.

SERC Examples

One example from SERC's portfolio is from Food Preparation Level 2 - Combatting food poverty in the local community. In this programme, the students work as part of a larger group tackling local food poverty by multi-agency support at a time of crisis.

The specific outcomes to be delivered include 2400 festive freshly-cooked healthy meals and education sessions on cooking healthy meals on a budget. The issues here include providing healthy high-quality food, support in preparing healthy food and empathy from SERC students and staff.

In their assessment tutors record the specific evidence against outcomes for each student including:

- **Problem solving** - Students tackle the logistics of providing suitable and nutritious meals, reducing waste in the kitchen, and providing basic cooking skills to the community.

- **Digital literacy** - Students evidence their work on the Food Poverty Project in their electronic portfolios to support their own studies. They use digital systems for improved recipe and culinary research, menu planning and design, communication and collaboration, online presence and marketing.

- **Work professionalism** - Students become working professionals and demonstrate essential industry skills, such as food safety and regulatory compliance in a real-world environment, project planning, costings, business-appropriate behaviour and evaluation skills.

- **Self-management** - Students are taken out of their comfort zone and taught how to think on their feet in different scenarios. Confidence, time-management, prioritisation and decisiveness are demonstrated in fast-paced and dynamic environments.

- **Working with others** - Students are taken out of their class bubbles and introduced to stakeholders in each project, including local councils, foodbanks, businesses, the media and charities. Student evaluations have also shown that they value working with students from different disciplines and backgrounds during social enterprise work.

- **Citizenship** - The development of social enterprise to support the community is widening student thought processes, creating empathetic and knowledgeable professionals with greater tolerance and understanding for others.

SERC has also noted that the Project-Based Learning approach requires careful planning at the start of the academic year. Curriculum teams need to work together to agree and plan the projects that students will do and how these map back to the qualification learning outcomes and assessment criteria.

An example of this is mapping for the Garden Room project described in Case Study 7.1. Planning allowed the lecturers to have confidence that the projects would satisfy the qualification assessment criteria. However, as part of the planning process, curriculum teams needed to consider whether there was adequate breadth and depth of T skills development across the projects, and whether amendments needed to be made to improve this.

In the case of the Garden Room project, lecturers used the OCNNI Level 2 Certificate in Transversal Skills to provide the learning outcomes for the projects. A formal qualification was used for two reasons:

- Transversal skills development is a specified component of the traineeship and the available evidence suggested that a systematic approach was needed to ensure adequate development of these skills.

- The current education and employment systems rely on qualifications to prove competence and learning. Change in this regard will take time, and so it was decided that a qualification would be the best way to evidence the learning while systematic change is pursued.

To expand on the first point, in the past it had been taken for granted that T skills would be developed as part of the learning process. However, employer feedback suggested that this was not always the case. The qualification provided a breakdown of what the skills meant at different performance levels, providing lecturers and students with goals and benchmarks. For example, Citizenship T skills include the learning outcome, "know how to apply the principles of social diversity", which includes assessment criteria such as: 'Apply the principles of social diversity through a group project involving at least one of the following: staff, peers and others'.

Trainees were able to demonstrate this as part of their group Garden Room project by showing respect to their peers who were from different social backgrounds and by demonstrating awareness of each other's needs and acceptable behaviour.

An Example of U Skill Assessment

As explained in Case Study 8.1, U skills are often needed in the Health and Social Care sector so, in that example, these were introduced with explanation, discussion and clear assessment criteria to allow students to self-assess. Students were supported in reflecting on where and how they had demonstrated U skills during their work experience, and in flagging this development with digital "tags" in their portfolio.For example, these are extracts from a supervisor assessment of student X:

'X was under my personal wing when she joined and I often got to observe how she coped, managed, and thrived in an environment which at times could present as very intense and demanding, requiring cool headedness and *critical decision-making*. She has been working exclusively with one person (J) that we support - a particular individual who was someone we believed X could be suited to and we are happy to see that this was a good match.

X had a natural calmness when it came to handling, supporting, and reassuring J when she presented with seizures, being neither phased nor deterred when she first encountered their strength and their frequency. X demonstrated her *emotional intelligence* by identifying where she was not confident and working on these points until she felt she had enough experience to demonstrate her knowledge to new staff. She asked for support with regards to finances and the running of the house, such as groceries and financial limitations, understanding that although her strengths lay in the social aspect of her job roles, that was only one part of what was expected. She listened to my advice when J presented with behaviours that were challenging, learning how to know when to give space and sit tight when appropriate. Now she can see that she is able to contribute to her team with her own suggestions and useful observations.

After frustration with the lack of clear information on the back of J's blister pack, X phoned the pharmacy several times to try and receive clearer labelling. The information, due to the quantity of meds that were required for distribution continued to dissatisfy X. She demonstrated her *entrepreneurial skills* by painstakingly looking up every med, writing and sketching a detailed picture and description, including the purpose, colour, size, shape, dosage and frequency for each tablet or capsule.

She took it upon herself to update this anytime there was a change in brand, dosage or med. Support staff reported that this was a very helpful visual aid, especially for those that were new to working alongside J. It also made it much easier to identify meds in the blister pack and see when something had changed.

X also strives to hold *professional values* and tries to look at different perspectives that she doesn't always agree with but will reflect on these experiences and will find learning in them.'

And these are extracts from the X's own evidence summary:

'Within *critical thinking* I believe I have shown interpretation and evaluation on my reflection after an anatomy and physiology class. This was completed on pact and can be found in reflective accounts. I interpretated and evaluated all I had learnt in that class and applied it to my future career as a paramedic as when learning about NEWS2 charts which I will see often as a paramedic.

This reflection allows me to think and understand what I am likely to be encountering during my career.

I believe I have demonstrated *emotional intelligence* when reflecting on my anatomy and physiology exam. I completed a written reflection upon receiving my grade. I reflected on what went well, what went bad and how to improve for future exams. I managed my emotions through evaluating how I felt with different areas of the exam. This badge can be found in the reflective accounts section. My reflection was overall positive experience, which helps to create a positive plan for moving forward with my learning.

When creating my smart goals which can be found in the professional principles tab, I feel I have shown *entrepreneurship* and *leadership*. I have used *creativity* and *innovation* and planning and management. This is due to my smart goals being planned precisely while remaining managed and targeted towards both my long-term and short term goals I have shown *creativity* and *innovation* when creating my goals and plan to ensure they are diverse and help me to meet my long-term goals and short-term goals within an efficient range of time, allowing me to pursue further goals.'

Other Benefits

It is also relevant to note that it was not just having an assessment that was helpful to students, but the process of assembling it was also found to be very beneficial. nitially, the Health and Social Care students were resistant to mapping their U skills to their evidence portfolios as they did not see the relevance of the activity. However, after discussion about the importance of U skills for employability and carer progression, and after reviewing some job descriptions and applications, the students were much more engaged. Indeed, many students appreciated that this activity would support them in applying and interviewing for jobs as it helped them to articulate and evidence their U skills, with one student in particular reporting that this had specifically helped her succeed in an interview.

References

1 T. Heywood in D. Matheson (Ed). An Introduction to the Study of Education, (London: Routledge, 2015 4th Edn) p.131

CHAPTER 10

T SKILLS DEVELOPMENT: A FURTHER EXAMPLE

Chapter Summary

SERC has not been the only educational organisation in Northern Ireland seeking to develop students' T skills. Young Enterprise has also been doing this.

While it has not used the same vocabulary to describe its efforts, it has used experiential learning and a reflective 'exam' to provide students with an assessment certificate.

Introduction

The description in Part II of SERC's approach to T and U skill development is one example of doing this in a further education setting.

While SERC's work in introducing T and U skills has addressed the problems of vocabulary, methods and assessment, it is not the only example of such relevant endeavours. Another example in the primary and post-primary school system in Northern Ireland is the work of the charity, Young Enterprise Northern Ireland.

Young Enterprise

Young Enterprise is part of Junior Achievement Worldwide, which operates in over 100 countries and reaches 15 million young people annually.

The network has been nominated three times for the Nobel Peace prize and advises international organisations such as the World Economic Forum on best practice in enterprise education. This allows Young Enterprise staff to benchmark practice, programme content and learn from others in the global community.

The experience of the charity, which has been working with education for over 30 years in Northern Ireland, demonstrates a clear appetite amongst educators for the use of project-based learning activities when there is space available in the curriculum to deliver. Young Enterprise maintains current with the needs of business by partnering with volunteers from local business and working with the wider business community to develop relevant programme content that supports educators to deliver for the needs of young people in their schools.

Alumni have stated that their experience helps them succeed at interviews and sets them apart from their peers in the workplace and 82% of young people say that taking part in Young Enterprise has given them confidence to succeed in the future.

Methods

The charity uses a methodology which has been developed over decades of supporting young people internationally to develop entrepreneurial skills for future employability. Students participate in practical skills-based activities with business mentors and can set up and run their own student companies, trading to the general public to develop practical experiences of skills.

This methodology allows students to practice skills using a project-based learning approach and can mean that learners have the opportunity to practice these skills multiple times during their education journey, prior to the high-stakes environment of the workplace where they are expected to be able to demonstrate expertise.

This focus on entrepreneurial skills for work-readiness contrasts with the strong emphasis on academic achievement that exists in the Northern Ireland education system. When students have the opportunity to experience these project-based learning techniques it provides a foundation of knowledge of skills that can be built upon as students transition into post primary and further education. The benefit of a curriculum that allows for skills development in this manner, means that where these programmes are delivered on a sequential basis, it can provide a strong foundation to achieve competence in skills before moving into the workplace.

At primary level, this is delivered on cross-curricular basis, allowing for application of skills such as English for business tasks such as marketing materials or maths for pricing. In post primary, the nature of subject-based curriculum delivery, makes the achievement of cross-curriculum skills development more challenging. Typically, the responsibility for skills development falls to careers departments or business studies, despite skills policy suggesting it should be a cross-curricular consideration. The statutory 'Learning for Life and Work' strand allows for project based activity in this space, and this is often where this learning will reside.

These entrepreneurial education experiences provide young people with the opportunity to practice skills and make mistakes through the project of running a business. It is rare that a business will go to plan, meaning students gain the opportunity to adapt and problem solve, perhaps even reframing failures into learning experiences.

An Enterprising Mindset

In 2023, Young Enterprise NI's parent body in the UK celebrated 60 years of what it described as helping to 'transform young people's lives through enterprise and financial education'. In particular, it pointed out that, through its Company Programme, 'young people are introduced to the realities of the world of work ... and develop an enterprising mindset' - which is said to have these 11 components:[1]

- Work readiness
- Organisation
- Aspiration
- Teamwork
- Confidence
- Creativity
- Problem solving
- Resilience
- Communication
- Financial capability
- Working responsibly

Although not labelled by Young Enterprise as such, these 11 components nevertheless have a lot in common with the lists of economically relevant T (and U) skill sets suggested at the end of chapter 3. Thus Young Enterprise has been assisting T skill development without using that label, bringing to mind the realisation of Molière's Bourgeois Gentilhomme that:

'I have been speaking prose all my life without knowing it.'

Assessment

Young Enterprise Northern Ireland has also added an assessment process to its Company Programme, usually undertaken in schools by sixth formers. This takes the form of an 'exam' supported by Ulster University in which participants reflect on the skills they have developed during the programme. This has been described by a teacher as 'valuable and meaningful for pupils to evaluate their journey' and all those who pass the exam receive a certificate to recognise their effective participation.

Summary

Thus, although not using the same vocabulary as SERC, Young Enterprise in Northern Ireland is an example of another educational organisation which has been developing young people's T skills through experiential learning and then, in some cases, providing a reflective assessment of their participation and achievement.

References

1 Young Enterprise, Company Programme Impact Report 2022-23, (London, Young Enterprise, 2014)

PART 3

FURTHER REFLECTIONS, IMPLICATIONS AND CONCLUSIONS

CHAPTER 11

RSTU SKILLS: SOME IMPLICATIONS AND CONCLUSIONS

Chapter Summary

Starting with expressed requirements for our education system to deliver employability, enterprise and entrepreneurship, this book has shown that these three Es will all be supported by a set of transversal skills which are also very relevant to other aspects of life.

This chapter reviews the barriers to the introduction of these T skills and higher-level U skills and the examples provided of how they can be overcome. It suggests, however, that such skills should not be seen as add-ons or exceptions to the normal education provision but as part of a new paradigm of what an education system should include.

Therefore, the book has not only offered a vocabulary for this but also a 'map' of a more complete system against which present provisions might be compared.

Introduction

The purpose of this book has been to suggest practical ways to improve our education system and made it more fit for the 21st century.

As Part I explains, the problems affecting education appear to be a 'complex' series of issues not related to just one aspect of it or the result of a single cause and effect process which can relatively easily be identified and corrected. Therefore, to address this fully, a combination of improvements is likely to be needed which will take time to develop and implement. However, this book tries to highlight important aspects which, it is becoming clearer, are not often adequately covered, and to suggest how a start might be made to include them.

Life and Work

The starting point for the discussions which led to this book was a shared awareness of various demands for education to deliver the three Es of 'employability', 'enterprise' and 'entrepreneurship' by preparing people better to be employable, to be enterprising generally or to start businesses.

However, there is no common consensus on the definitions of, and distinctions between, employability, enterprise and entrepreneurship in this context - and consequently there has been no clear agreement on how to deliver them. Therefore, as the book attempts to show, rather than consider each of the Es as leading to a supposedly distinct and mutually exclusive outcome, it is more helpful to view those outcomes as three possible pathways, any or all of which might be followed by someone trying to navigate life.

One of the issues highlighted is that the world of work is changing with long-term job opportunities in large organisations becoming rarer and changing jobs and self-employed working becoming more common. Therefore, subject knowledge or particular task or vocational skills are no longer alone sufficient and, both for work and for other aspects of life, a set of skills are needed to equip people to apply their knowledge and vocational skills in real and changing situations.

These component skills are transferable in that they can usefully be applied in a number of different situations - and therefore have been called Transversal (T) skills or, for the higher-level ones, Uber (U) skills. They are the foundation needed for success in life and work, especially when change and uncertainty are often the norm and whether that work is done as an employee or is self-driven.

As the map in Figure 5.1 attempts to show, these T and U skills do not replace S learning but instead enable its application in people lives. However, they are not like standard S learning as they are not fundamentally based on acquired knowledge. Nevertheless, and despite the economic incentive, education in them should not be seen as a separate, stand-alone issue and things related to it treated as a special and separate category of 'business' matters. Just as people need to eat in order to live, but do not live just to eat, so jobs and businesses are a key part of many people's lives but not their life aim. Similarly, the need for T and U skills may have been highlighted because of their work applications but that is only one part of their much wider relevance to people's lives.

The Barriers to including T Skills

T and U skills, however defined, are not a theoretical topic that can solely be taught by imparting knowledge: they are about practice and application and they form and develop overtime.

Young people need multiple opportunities to practice skills of all types to become competent. Time is required to understand the need for skills, to practise them, to make mistakes and learn, before they can build competency.

This book has therefore considered T and U skills and the need to include them in our education provision. It shows that they matter but that, nevertheless, demand for them often seems to be undervalued or ignored, not least because it is hampered by a number of factors, including:

- Ignorance of what these skills are and why they are needed - compounded by the lack of a shared vocabulary with which to describe them.

- A failure to understand where and at what stage they could or should fit into the current system.

- The lack of widely understood ways to 'deliver and assess' them as they are not knowledge based like standard school subjects and, more like sports, are best acquired through coached practice.

- The absence of accepted ways to measure their acquisition, which means they are not valued by, or on behalf of, their recipients as they do not lead to them gaining recognised 'qualifications'.

To try to help with the first of these obstacles, the book aims to introduce, explain, examine and to use a relevant vocabulary both to help identify what is missing and as a medium through with to discuss it.

However, having common labels for the missing skills does not itself initiate their introduction, especially if they cannot be 'taught' in classrooms like other school subjects. Therefore, in Part II, this book describes the practical example of SERC in its endeavours to impart T and U skills through Project Based Learning, showing both how those skills can be addressed and how their acquisition can be assessed. The summary of Young Enterprise's endeavours in chapter 10 then shows that SERC is not alone in this.

A New Paradigm

These examples show that T and U skills can and should be included in an education provision but awareness of that is more the beginning of a journey than its end. Realising that a change is needed does not automatically indicate what that change should be and how it might be effected.

There is sometimes a temptation to accept things which do not fit a prevailing view as recognised exceptions, often even as 'exceptions with prove the rule', or to make alterations to a process slowly by small increments which do not upset established systems and attract little resistance. Alternatively, a complete change can be attempted replacing an old and much criticised system with an apparently attractive new one - if such a one exists. But a new system often has not had its faults identified and removed - so a sudden and complete switch may not be an overall improvement.

Therefore, what is required is a measured and deliberate change of paradigm. The nature and relevance of T (and U) skills is being highlighted so that they and their relevance can be understood better - and case study examples of their teaching application and assessment are provided as a guide to their introduction. Although pressure from economic policy may have led to the advocation of employability, enterprise and/or entrepreneurship education, and then to the T skills upon which they appear to be based, those T skills, once understood, are clearly applicable to much of modern life. They were acquired by people in the past, but often as a consequence of the practice of life and not through deliberate instruction - and thus they were not necessarily acquired thoroughly or comprehensively. But life today needs T skills as well as the knowledge-based S learning that the education system has been accustomed to build - and therefore it would be advantageous to include them deliberately in the education system. It is hoped that this book can provide an impetus for that.

T skills are advocated as a response to the demands of modern life and in particular for economic contributions. They are a necessary foundation for being employable, for being enterprising and for starting a business, but new business creation requires in addition some process understanding. T skills also need to be taught by doing, for example, through Project Based Learning (PBL), but that will not happen without the motivation to do it - which might come from a new perspective or paradigm.

That perspective is summarised in the 'map' in Figure 5.1 which is intended to show examples of four categories of skill that people are likely to need for a fulfilling life. Traditionally, the formal education system has focussed on R proficiencies and S learning - leaving people to pick up T and sometimes U skills from their other activities. That was, however, a rather 'hit and miss' way to acquire them and now their inclusion in official education is increasingly being requested or required.

Also, there are many possible T and U skills and the skill sets suggested are just one way of grouping those which might be the most relevant. However, the suggestions made are not final or perfect and different combinations are possible - so others should try to build better on these suggestions. But the suggested vocabulary, delivery and assessment methods are offered as a starting point.

Those who wait for a perfect solution to copy will wait a long time. If there is any merit in the examples in this book then the way for an institution to make progress is to start the change, and not to assign it to an individual or small team, but to involve everyone in developing the approaches along the lines suggested. After all, it is by such methods that all good ideas are turned into useful reality.

Further Reflections

From its explorations of the changes necessary in education, this book also offers some further reflections:

- What should be the prime aim here? Are the three Es being viewed from a people or an economic development perspective? Is their inclusion in education primarily to prepare students for life or to enhance their contribution to economic development?

- If the prime aim is to help prepare for life, then the book suggests that T and U skills are essential. However, until T and U skills are viewed as important as exam passes in traditional subjects (S learning) will they be valued?

- If the prime aim is economic development, by means such as increasing the number of start-ups, then T and U skills are still needed but business start-up requires some additional specific process understanding.

- However, if the aim is more business start-ups, the evidence suggests that teaching (and supporting) enterprise for new venture creation will not deliver that and instead social influence is likely to be the main factor.

Therefore, it is suggested that there are lessons in this for:

- Education providers - schools, FE and HE.
- Education consumers - students and those guiding them.
- Education policy makers and implementers.
- Economic policy makers - especially advocates of 'entrepreneurship'.

It is hoped that this book can contribute to an evolving understanding of this important area but it is not the end. Recognising the need for change does not immediately lead to a definitive and complete alternative - but it does suggest a need to look and the thoughts in this book are offered to try to aid that search.

Index